MW01587004

Walking the HighWire

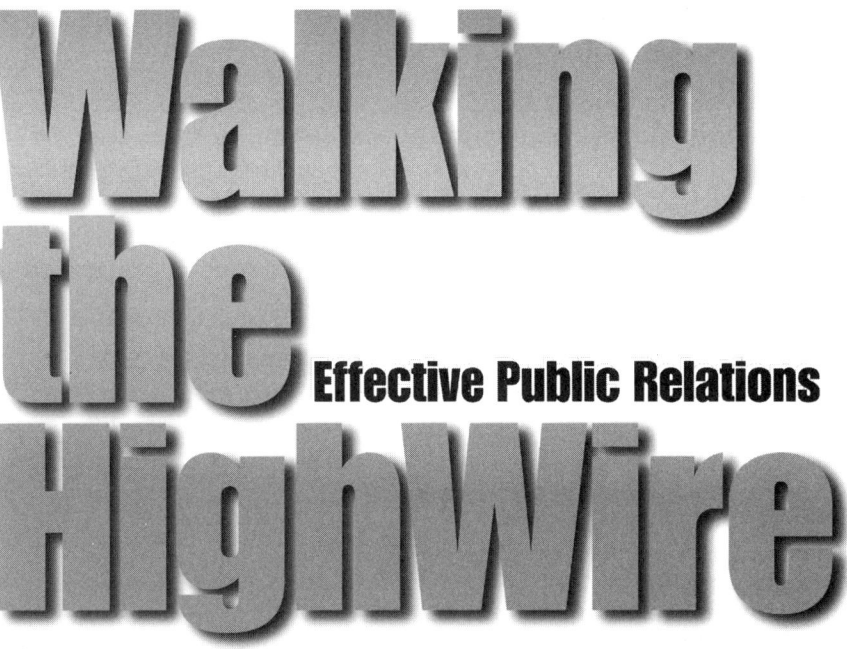

Walking the HighWire

Effective Public Relations

Merry Clare Shelburne
Glendale Community College

coursewise
publishing
inc.

Boulder • Bellevue • Dubuque • Madison

Our mission at CourseWise is to help students make connections—linking theory to
practice and the classroom to the outside world. Learners are motivated to synthesize ideas when course
materials are placed in a context they recognize. By providing gateways to contemporary and enduring
issues, CourseWise publications will expand students' awareness of and context for the course subject.

For more information on CourseWise visit us at our web site: www.coursewise.com

CourseWise Publishing Editorial Staff

Thomas Doran, ceo/publisher: Journalism/Marketing
Edgar Laube, publisher: Geography/Political Science/Psychology/Sociology/Speech
Linda Meehan Avenarius, publisher: CourseLinks
Victoria Putman, publisher: Anthropology/Philosophy/Religion
Sue Pulvermacher-Alt, publisher: Education/Health/Physical Education/Women's Studies
Tom Romaniak, publisher: Business/Criminal Justice/Economics

Other CourseWise Journalism publications
Journalism 2001 by Christopher Harper and the Indiana Group
Perspectives, On-Line Journalism edited by Kathleen Wickham

Back cover photo: Author Merry Shelburne and Prince Fuzzibear O'Hara

Interior design, cover design, and cover art Jeff Storm

Copyright © 1998 by CourseWise Publishing, Inc. All rights reserved

ISBN 0-395-898773

No part of this publication may be reproduced, stored in a retrieval system, or transmitted,
in any form or by any means, electronic, mechanical, photocopying, recording, or otherwise,
without the prior written permission of the publisher.

Printed in the United States of America by CourseWise Publishing, Inc.
1379 Lodge Lane, Boulder, CO 80303

10 9 8 7 6 5 4 3 2

To Dave

Contents

Preface

Walking the HighWire: Effective Public Relations is a textbook/workbook designed for prospective public relations experts.

It is a practical instruction manual appropriate for business school students, PR or journalism majors enrolled in their first two years of college, upper division university students seeking an overall survey of PR practices, or those whose goals are to become PR professionals for business or charity purposes.

HighWire is reality-based. It provides in logical sequence the knowledge necessary for effective public relations practices, encourages critical thinking and writing skills, and explains the common-sense psychological and sociological reasoning upon which recommended actions are based.

It also covers the up-to-date technological aspects of cyberPR, from alert faxes to telepress conferences to web sites.

The author has been a successful PR practitioner since the 70s, has a background in the media and has taught many journalism courses. Her recommendations are based on experience rather than theory, and her writing style is a departure from the usual stuffy textbook verbiage.

HighWire is a personal communication between the author and the student, and therefore a user-friendly teaching text rather than just an informational book. Enjoy!

Acknowledgments

This book is dedicated to the author's husband, Dave, whose love, encouragement, patience and advice provided the psychological crutch necessary for stamina and perseverance.

A special thanks goes to Mom, who opened her checkbook more than once and who, as Moms often do, gave advice freely.

The author also wishes to thank her nephews, Brian, Jerry, Bart and Jimmy Delbridge, in-laws, friends and work mates for all their encouragement and enthusiasm; journalism mentor Joe G. Thomas; Don Johnson (not the movie star), who designed the CyberChow logo and provided other desk-top assistance; Susan Cisco for photographic assistance; and the news organizations that supplied free photos: KABC talk radio Los Angeles, and the Daily News of Los Angeles.

Finally, the author owes a big thanks to publisher Tom Doran for his faith, enthusiasm, and cutting-edge ideas.

Section One

Preparation

What Is Public Relations?

Public relations has nearly as many definitions as there are people who have tried to define it.

An over-simplified version voiced by one PR practitioner was "Planned Reaction." But that definition is inaccurate because it's impossible to *plan* the public's reaction to anything. You can use common sense and attempt to provoke a reaction to a certain stimulus, but nothing is assured in the practice of public relations.

As a matter of fact, the above-mentioned PR person is now out of business . . . probably due to a failure to understand basic PR principles.

A more realistic working definition is: The continuous effort to persuade the mass media to deliver messages that will enhance your organization/company/client's public image.

Yes, it's that tenuous.

Successful PR requires a thorough understanding of the mass media and those employed in the media. It also takes healthy doses of common sense and imagination. Organization and communication skills are vital, as is a knowledge of psychology and sociology. And all that might not be enough without some control over the actions and words of your client or organization's leaders.

This profession requires a person who is intelligent, can function under stress, is not prone to temper tantrums, has no ego, is sensitive to other people's feelings and can move quickly.

Still interested? Then here's one more piece of information: Even if you have all the required knowledge and skills, there's no guarantee you'll get a *planned reaction*. That's why our definition begins with, ". . .continuous effort to persuade . . ."

Just A Little History

The most important aspect of PR history is that the profession's practitioners traditionally have been viewed with skepticism and mistrust. Ergo, thanks to your predecessors, you will have to deal with that poor image. Ironic, isn't it? You will be working hard to enhance your company's image—and succeeding—even though the PR industry universally is considered somewhat . . . less than desirable. The only way to erase that image is for an entire generation of PR professionals to act responsibly and ethically.

How did it all begin? The concept of public relations did not really emerge in this country until the mass media were invented. Before then, "public relations" consisted of store owners trying to please their customers and politicians attempting to influence their constituents.

But once the industrial revolution was underway and railroads spread across the nation, companies were eager to expand and sell their wares to customers outside their immediate vicinity.

In the 1830s, several competing "Penny Press" newspapers were established in New York City. The new concept was to sell papers for a penny and rely on advertising monies to support the publication. And magazines followed the concept shortly thereafter. Ah, advertising. It was the beginning.

Soon, company officials began to see that a good product and clever advertising were not always enough to bring customers flocking to their stores. Something more was needed—reputation, image, public opinion. Once the chiefs grasped that concept, the door was open for men (and it was MEN) who believed they could alter a company's image by changing the public's collective mind.

Thus began the trial-and-error practice of "public relations." And since most politicians were also businessmen, they hired PR "flacks" to help their campaigns. After all, wouldn't public opinion affect how people voted just as much as it affected where people bought their clothes? Unfortunately for all of you today who may be considering a PR career, those *flacks* pulled every underhanded trick they could think of to get their men elected. It was the start of the "department of dirty tricks," and that's your legacy.

Things got worse. By the time World War I rolled around, some of those politicians were in Washington, and they had brought their PR people with them. The practice of trying to control public opinion had become much more sophisticated and widespread. Now, newspapers and magazines were everywhere, giving access to most people across the country. The U.S. government made use of the press by firing up patriotism and convincing citizens that America should join the war.

Radio arrived on the scene and provided another, more instantaneous media outlet. And as soon as most Americans had radio sets, attempts to fiddle with public opinion became more and more prevalent. The president's speeches and "fireside chats" could be heard by everyone at once, and the movie industry attracted audiences by publicizing films and stars. The movie industry. . . . More flacks. Only this time it wasn't so much dirty tricks as it was vivid imaginations and publicity stunts. No wonder the PR profession developed a bad name.

Television hit its stride after World War II, and with it came almost unlimited opportunities to influence public opinion. Here was a medium that captured the ears AND the eyes of the nation. PR practitioners in other fields were joining their colleagues in politics and the film industry, and PR firms began to flourish and spread the profession to other parts of the Western world.

Then came the turbulent decade that began the day John F. Kennedy was assassinated in 1963 and more or less ended the day Richard M. Nixon resigned in 1974. For the first time, television brought shocking, frightening and confusing images into the living room of every home. The Vietnam War. Long-haired rock and roll bands and loud music. Student demonstrations. Riots in the ghettos. Man walking on the moon. Anti-war demonstrations. Hippies and flower children. Kent State. Drugs. The assassinations of Robert F. Kennedy and Dr. Martin Luther King. Woodstock. Watergate. The parents of the baby-boomer generation were shaken to the core, courtesy of TV, and the PR industry was ineffective in controlling the outrage. The more TV covered, the more frightened adults became and the more tuned-in young people were to the activities of their peers. The government was powerless to stem the tide, and public opinion eventually forced an end to the war and a reluctant acceptance of boomer sensibilities.

The PR industry learned, grew and became more sophisticated in its attempts to manipulate public opinion through the media. Entire countries such as South Africa

KTLA Morning News anchors Carlos Amezcua & Barbara Beck host a show that's a perfect vehicle for public relations practitioners to promote their clients.
Photo courtesy of the Daily News of Los Angeles

hired PR firms to handle their images. "Spin doctors" (not to be confused with the rock band) emerged in politics to *schmooze* reporters and the public. Words like *schmooze* entered the vocabulary.

And that's pretty much where we stand today.

Now. . .

There are legions of legitimate PR practitioners serving as Public Information Officers and public relations experts for organizations and companies, but the flacks are still around—still up to their dirty tricks and publicity stunts.

If the latter type of PR people weren't somewhat successful in fooling the public, their breed would die out. But it would be best for society if they would open their eyes and find a way to emulate the folks at Tylenol. During the 1980s that company suffered an image disaster—someone had poisoned its pills. Instead of making excuses, hiding and sniveling, trying a cover-up and diversionary tactics or pointing fingers at others, Tylenol reps IMMEDIATELY inundated the media with announcements. They said, in essence: We feel terrible about this! We're much more concerned about the health of our customers than we are about making money, so we insist you destroy or return to the store for a refund all Tylenol products. We think it was just a few of one type of pill, but we don't want you to take any chances. We promise we won't return Tylenol to the shelf until we can insure your safety. And we'll work tirelessly with law enforcement to find the culprit and develop more security measures.

That approach was a public relations triumph! It fostered TRUST, which is what a pharmaceutical company needs more than anything else to survive. Today, Tylenol dominates its industry. Kudos to the PR expert who ran the show and provided an example to us all.

Case Study

At the end of most chapters, you will find an actual case study relating to the section's topic. These situations were experienced by the author since 1977 as the Public Information Officer at Glendale Community College in California. Minor details and names have been omitted to protect the innocent and/or guilty, but the stories are true. We hope these examples will further clarify the points we are trying to make and also provide some additional insight into the real world of public relations.

Related Web Sites

In lieu of the usual "Recommended Readings" that traditionally appear at the end of college textbook chapters, we have provided a new feature: web sites where students might surf for expanded information or see examples of good public relations. Enjoy.

www.nike.com
www.goarmy.com
www.lexus.com
www.virtually.com

chapter one
EXERCISES

Name_____ **Date**_____

1. Write down your own definition of public relations and an explanation of the importance of ethics. Be prepared to discuss and defend it in class. (When you have finished reading WALKING THE TIGHTROPE, go back and look at your early assessment and see if it has changed).

2. Bring to class a newspaper story that's an example of good public relations. Be prepared to discuss why it's good PR and what the company or organization gained from the story.

3. Find a web site (other than the ones listed at the conclusions of these chapters) you think is an example of good public relations. Write a short essay defending your choice, and don't forget to describe the site.

Name_____ **Date** _____

4. Watch a local TV newscast and find a story that exemplifies good public relations. Write a description of the story and tell why it was good PR and what the company or organization gained from it.

5. Find a story in a newspaper or on a TV newscast that you think was beneficial to the company or organization. Contact the company and speak to its public relations person. Ask what the PR person did, if anything, to promote the story. Write a short essay about your experience.

Chapter 2

Types of PR Jobs and Activities

An almost limitless variety of public relations jobs exist and more are being invented daily. They run the gamut from Vice President of Marketing to publicity chair for the local women's club. It could be argued that the most powerful PR person in the country is the President's press secretary, but it's more likely that position is held by the marketing VP in some multinational conglomerate. Money makes the world go 'round.

If you do harbor a secret ambition to grab one of those White House press office jobs, be prepared for one of the most challenging experiences of your life. The daily fare is pressure, with regular doses of confusion, exhilaration, frustration and exhaustion.

But let us return to reality and positions more readily available. We'll start at the top of that PR world and work our way down the ladder, looking at the possibilities on each rung.

The Biz

Big Guys

A multinational corporation's marketing VP would be responsible for the company's public image and would attempt to manipulate that image through both advertising and public relations techniques. The same would hold true for a large U.S.-held corporation, which also is big enough to have its own marketing department.

Then, of course, there are all those middle-management types, artists and writers, secretaries and clerks, commercial producers, camera operators, still photographers, videotape editors, etc., who are employed by those marketing departments.

International and U.S. public relations firms also occupy positions of power because frequently they are employed by—for example—nations, cities, politicians, the entertainment industry, and, yes, the multinational conglomerates and U.S. companies that do not have in-house PR departments. These firms might be responsible for hiring an advertising agency, or they might simply coordinate their efforts with such an agency. Again, PR companies utilize the skills of artists and writers, still photographers, etc., which provide places for you to get your foot on the first rung of the corporate ladder.

A word should be said here about polling and survey companies. They are hired to scientifically test public opinion about various issues (usually political). But because the media almost always reveal the results of those surveys, the polls become sort of self-fulfilling prophecies because they, in turn, influence public opinion. Ergo, survey companies occupy a powerful position in the public relations business. Jobs in this industry are less creative and more oriented toward designing polling questions, selecting proper random samples and accurately tabulating the results.

First lady Hillary Rodham Clinton makes an appearance at KABC Talk Radio.
Photo by Bill Lennert

Smaller Companies

Medium-sized companies frequently have a public relations department, and the smaller the company the smaller the department. PR officers in this scenario would handle a variety of tasks, including media relations, internal communication, and perhaps publications and advertising coordination. The number of tasks and work load usually determine the number of staff in the PR office, but positions could include administrator, writer, artist, photographer/videocam operator, typesetter or graphics publications specialist and clerk/secretary.

Smaller PR firms and freelance practitioners handle the overflow—sometimes augmenting a PR department's efforts or replacing that office altogether. Cities and small businesses frequently hire local PR companies to help with campaigns or ongoing projects, and these companies typically hire multitalented employees who can take on a variety of tasks.

It should be noted here that the newest field is cybercopywriting and all the attendant possibilities. For a thorough discussion, see Chapter 18.

Non-Profit

Moving out of corporate America, we find ample PR opportunities in non-profit organizations, educational institutions, governmental entities, and, somewhere between private and public, hospitals. Depending on the size of the organization, the PR office could be quite extensive or just a one-person setup. Typically, these PR practitioners are called Public Information Officers or Community Relations Officers or some hybrid of the two. The concept behind these titles is to invoke the image of a helpful person just handing out information rather than someone scheming to alter public opinion. For instance, at the scene of a large fire, media usually can find a person wearing firefighter gear and a helmet with big "PIO" letters on it. That means he or she is available to give interviews and provide all the latest information.

Finally, there are volunteer PR jobs—usually with local clubs seeking publicity for an upcoming event.

Duties

Depending on the emphasis your organization places on the importance of public relations, you could be working solo—even part-time—or you could be part of a large staff.

But no matter what, your number one duty is to deal with the media. Except for direct mail campaigns or the internet, without the press you cannot reach the public. Effective media relations requires a thorough understanding of that industry, persuasive skills and the ability to communicate verbally and in writing. Details of those tasks are discussed in chapters 3 and 4 and Section 2.

You also might be responsible for company publications, either external or internal. For this task you'll need good writing skills, a knowledge of desktop publishing systems, the ability to take pictures or draw illustrations, and familiarity with the printing process—or at least have staff members who can do all those things.

Another possibility is advertising. You might need to write and even produce radio ads or public service announcements. You might be required to produce TV commercials. You might have to design and produce camera-ready newspaper ads. Or you might even be coordinating a PR campaign with advertising. This all takes a great deal of creativity and probably the ability to work with others in a cooperative manner.

Case Study

As the Public Information Officer at Glendale Community College, my responsibilities run the PR gamut. My office handles all media relations, all publications, both print and broadcast advertising, sports information, original artwork, calligraphy, the speakers bureau, and many unexpected duties that regularly are thrown at us at the last minute. I say "us" because my staff consists of an editorial assistant, a graphic artist, and a typesetter/desktop publishing expert. We have several recurring projects —such as class schedules, college catalog, and various sports media guides—but the rest of it can best be described as "Surprise!" Each day is a challenge, and that's what we love about it. No dull repetition here.

The skills we all share include a thorough knowledge of proper grammar, a certain artistic sense, varying degrees of computer literacy, and, most importantly, a SENSE OF HUMOR. You can't be in PR and not laugh at the absurdities surrounding you. And we also spend some time each day making fun of ourselves. It's a healthy, cobweb-clearing practice.

Overlapping skills include media relations proficiency, writing, photography, sports knowledge, freehand artwork, desktop, videotaping and editing, advertising strategies, tact, internet surfing, and the ability to keep a straight face when someone asks us to "put this in the paper." Overlapping means some of us can, and one or more can't. For example, I can do everything except complex desktop and original artwork, but no one else knows how to edit videotape. (Actually, I draw pretty good stick figures, but that's another story.)

The point is, we work as a team, and each of us is invaluable. I couldn't survive without any of them, and (I like to think) they'd be rudderless without me.

We are proudest of the fact that we achieve good media coverage and the college enjoys an excellent reputation, despite the fact that the PIO has a miniscule operating budget. For example, at press time our advertising expenditures were less than $10,000 annually.

To provide a setting for my office, let me explain that Glendale College has 14,000 college credit students and another 8,000 non-credit enrollees at sites mostly off the main campus. We are located just 10 minutes from Los Angeles and must compete for media attention with every kind of entertainment, sports activity, and university imaginable. There are 106 community colleges in California and nearly 20 in Los Angeles County, and we're convinced they all have larger budgets than we do. Ha. Ha.

Related Web Sites
www.Yahoo.com/Business_and_Economy/Companies/Corporate_Services/Public_Relations/
www.akleinpr.com
www.hillandknowlton.com
www.webpr.com
www.bayne.com/wolfBayne

Those are the major categories of public relations jobs, but there are many other aspects of the business that require additional skills and responsibilities. For instance, you might have to compile sports statistics or operate a speakers bureau. You might have to design surveys or organize a political campaign. You might have to develop a city's public relations plan or ghost-write speeches. You might have to participate in fundraising activities or engage in public speaking. You might have to lobby legislators or work on research projects. The possibilities are endless. Anything even remotely related to public relations, and sometimes things that aren't, may be thrown your way.

In PR, one of the keys to success is an understanding of how the communication process works, both on a personal level and in the mass media arena. Communication flow is covered in the next chapter.

chapter two

EXERCISES

Name_____ **Date**_____

1. What skills would you need to be a successful Public Information Officer for a metropolitan police department, and why?

2. Contact a large public relations firm and interview a high-ranking executive. Find out about that person's duties and climb to the top rung. Write a short essay about what you have learned.

Name_____ **Date** _____

3. Contact a large corporation and interview the public relations executive. Find out about that person's responsibilities and background. Write a short essay about what you have learned.

4. Contact a publicist for entertainment or sports figures and interview that person about the job. Ask about duties and background, and write a short essay about what you have learned.

Name_____   **Date** _____

5. Contact a large non-profit organization and interview the public relations person. In a short essay, compare that person's responsibilities with those of a PR practitioner at a private company.

6. Contact the public relations specialist for your city, police or fire department. Find out if, or how, that person interacts with those in the other two departments, and write a short essay on the subject.

Chapter **3**

How Communication Works

Social scientists have been trying to understand the communication process for years. They've experimented, they've tested, they've drawn diagrams. As it stands now, they agree about some elements and disagree on others. This chapter will be devoted to the particulars on which the experts currently agree.

We will not dwell on past theories that have been proven false and discarded, except for the so-called hypodermic model—just to prove a point. There was a time when social scientists believed mass communication consisted of delivering a message to the public and the public receiving and understanding the message exactly as it was sent— somewhat like giving someone a booster shot. That theory was incorrect because it did not take into consideration all the INTERFERENCE inherent in any communication process.

If you're going to be a communication specialist, you have to know these things. Right?

Interpersonal Communication

The simple components of the communication process between two individuals are the ENCODER (person sending the message), the MESSAGE, the VEHICLE or MEDIUM by which the message is transported, and the DECODER (person receiving the message). (*See Fig. 3.1*)

For example, John and Mary are standing three feet apart, face-to-face in the office coffee room. Mary decides to tell John she likes his tie. She says, "I like your tie." She is the ENCODER, the person who creates and sends the MESSAGE, "I like your tie." The VEHICLE by which the message is sent is her voice. John hears her say, "I like your tie," thus becoming the DECODER, or the person who has received the message.

Seems simple enough, doesn't it? It isn't. Let's consider the possibilities for physical and psychological interference.

Suppose the radio was blasting in the coffee room, and John couldn't hear Mary say, "I like your tie?" Suppose there were other people in the room, and Mary was looking over John's shoulder when she said, "I like your tie?" He might think she was speaking to someone else. Suppose John was preoccupied with a work problem or wasn't feeling well, and Mary spoke in a whisper? The fact that she spoke might not register with him at all. Suppose John was a secret admirer?

Bob Hope shows his communication skills as he emcees KTLA's first telecast in 1947.
Photo courtesy of the Daily News of Los Angeles

21

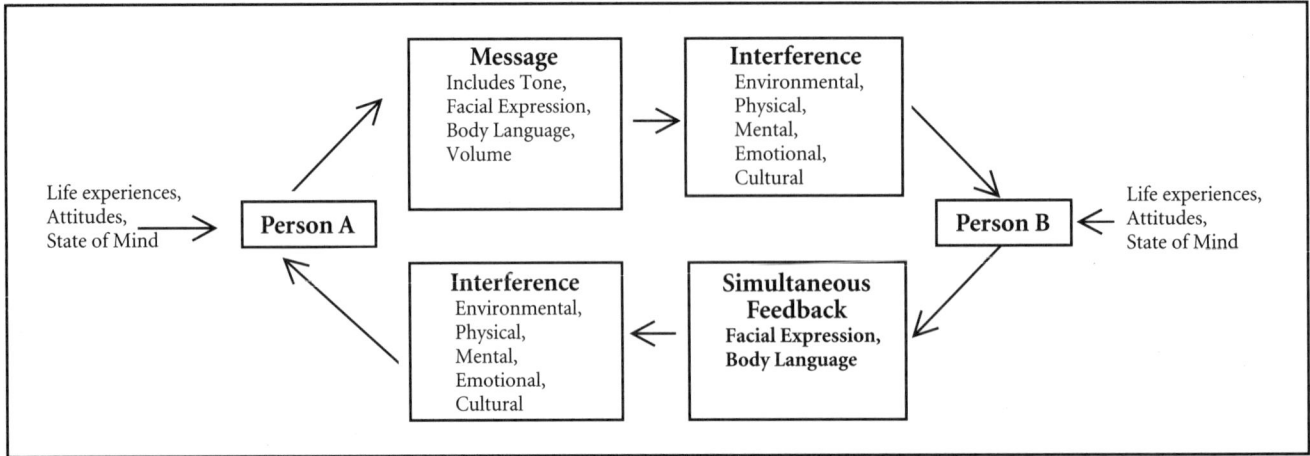

Figure 3.1
Face-to-face personal
communication model

There would be a difference in the way he interpreted her statement if she looked him in the eye and smiled—or looked at something else and bustled past him. Body language and facial expressions play a big role in the communication process. Suppose Mary was being sarcastic, but John chose to interpret her words as a compliment?

The possibilities for interference are limitless . . . just in this one-way example. And it gets much more complicated when you add the response to the equation. There's always a response of some kind, even if the decoder didn't hear the message or realize he had been addressed. In that case John would go about his business, and that counts as a response.

And the moment the decoder responds to the message, he becomes an encoder, because he has formulated and sent a message. Thus, John becomes the ENCODER and Mary the DECODER when she receives John's MESSAGE. The VEHICLE or MEDIUM depends on John's response. He might shrug or smile. He might say, "Thank you" or "Really?" or "What?" He might look around to see if she was speaking to someone else. He might ignore her. The method of getting that message to Mary might be body language, facial expression or the spoken word. And, again, the possibilities for interference are endless. Make up your own.

What does all this mean to public relations specialists? It means you must be aware of potential interference and guard against it when you communicate with members of the media or your co-workers. Otherwise, your message could be garbled, or misinterpreted, or not received at all. This goes for written communication as well as phone conversations and face-to-face discussions. It also means you must pay close attention when you are the decoder and make sure you are receiving messages the way they are meant.

Actually, face-to-face is the easiest because you have the advantage of watching the other person's body language and facial expressions. These elements, along with the tone of the verbal response, are called FEEDBACK and they will give you clues to whether or not your message is being received as you meant it. Eye contact is vital. Not only does it help your powers of observation, it also gives you the appearance of being an honest person who is really listening and paying attention.

Written communication can be difficult because there is no immediate feedback, but you do have time to rethink your words and consider the possibilities of misinterpretation. Make sure the words and phrases you use are appropriate for (will be understood by) your audience.

Phone conversations probably are the most difficult because you can't see the other person and you don't have time for a rewrite. However, if you listen carefully, tone and inflection in the other person's voice will provide feedback.

Mass Communication

Mass communication takes place when an individual or one medium attempts to deliver a message to a vast audience that usually is not present. (An exception would be a concert, where all the principals are present but the "conversation" is mostly one-way).

We say, ". . . attempts to deliver . . ." because interference is truly limitless in this situation.

The components of the mass communication process are far more complex because there's no immediate feedback, if any, and almost insurmountable potential for physical, cultural and psychological interference. (*See Fig. 3.2*)

Initially the ENCODER is not always a single person. It could be a group, and that could mean disagreement about the message. In addition, encoders bring with them conscious and subconscious psychological and cultural attitudes, biases and preconceptions. These elements shape the content and form of the MESSAGE, as does the choice of medium.

Many MEDIUMS exist for delivering messages. There are radio and television programs and radio and TV commercials. There are newspaper and magazine articles and ads. There are billboards, books, web sites and direct mail. There are photographs, movies and music. Every day we are inundated with thousands of messages, which can influence our attitudes.

For advertising purposes, mediums are chosen based on access to target audiences. If, for example, you wanted to promote a new line of jeans for young men, you might choose MTV or *Rolling Stone* magazine. More typically, there is little choice of medium because the encoder already works for a newspaper or writes screenplays.

In subtotal, we have an encoder whose cultural and psychological makeup influence the CONTENT of the message and a medium that influences the FORM of the message. So we have interference already, but nothing compared to what's coming.

Interference

Every medium has built-in physical interference. For broadcasting, it takes the form of static, "snow", interruptions in cable service or technical breakdowns at local and network stations. For print, a page could be torn or the type smeared or the publication misplaced. Billboards can be obscured by heavy rain, direct mail can be lost or destroyed, and the film reel can break at the movie house.

Then there is physical interference from the audience. The vacuum cleaner in the next room could drown out a TV or radio show. A phone call could interrupt reading, or a flat tire could prevent attendance at a film opening. Endless possibilities.

But the biggest roadblock to receiving the message as intended comes from inside the (decoder) audience member's head. Despite demographic testing of target audiences and attempts to put viewers, readers and listeners into neat little groups with preordained responses, there's no guarantee the message will have the desired result.

Each person, despite similarities with other members of the same demographic group, is an individual. And an individual brings to every mass communication experience a whole lifetime of unique psychological, sociological and cultural preconceptions. This causes the person to use the senses selectively . . . reading this but

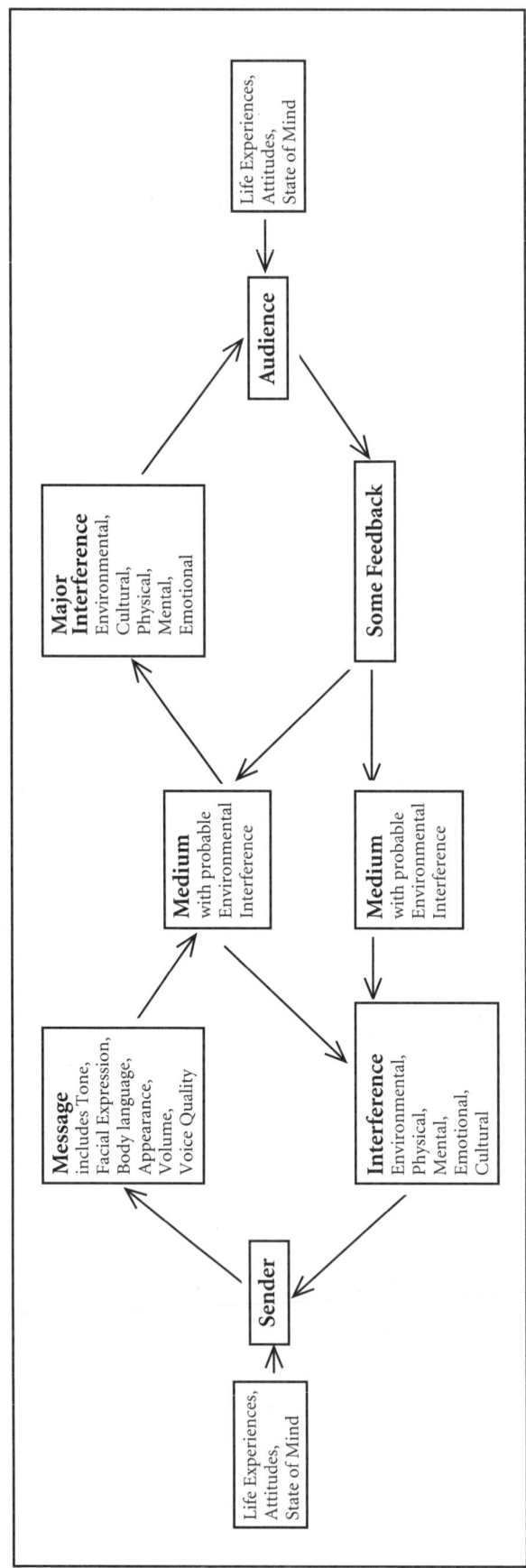

Figure 3.2
Mass communication model

Case Study

One of the oddest communication problems the PIO has at Glendale College is dealing with people who assume we already know about an event they want promoted. Although this happens infrequently, it's very frustrating. College professors, in particular, sometimes have a tendency to be somewhat absent-minded, and I guess we can't change human nature.

For example, someone calls and demands to know why pre-publicity for an event has not appeared in the campus weekly bulletin or the local newspapers. Let's say it's a presentation by a guest lecturer. Of course, they've forgotten to inform us about it:

"What guest lecturer?"
"Oh. Didn't I tell you about him?"
"No."
"Oh."

It's even more amusing when they forget to ask us to take pictures at a luncheon, or whatever it is, and then we get a panic call at the last minute. "Why isn't so-and-so here with her camera?" Invariably the person with the camera—there are two of us—is unavailable at that moment. Then the conversation goes something like this:

"Oh. Didn't we tell you we wanted pictures?"
"No."
"Oh. Well, can she come right now?"
"She's off campus. What did you want to use the pictures for?"
"Uh, we might use them in a newsletter or something."

(Many times we're asked to take pictures at events that are not particularly photo-worthy. We suspect some of these pix are for private albums rather than school business, but we try to accommodate people anyway.)

Seriously, a lack of communication is the biggest problem in any organization. Talk about interference!

Related Web Sites

www.jou.ufl.edu/commres/jouwww.htm
www.cais.com/makulow/vlj.html#cc
www.future.sri.com:80/vals/valshome.html

not that, believing this and discarding that, not seeing this and imagining that. Then there are short attention spans, boredom, anger, hunger . . . All of these things short-circuit the communication process.

There is feedback, of a kind, in mass communication. Letters to the editor, phone calls or telegrams to the station, low attendance at a movie. But the feedback usually arrives too late to alter the original message.

The bottom line is there's strong interference or the potential for interference every step of the way in the mass communication process. This means messages frequently are not received as intended, or received at all, which in turn means professional communicators must work harder to drive around the roadblocks.

As a PR practitioner, you must always take into careful consideration your AUDIENCE. How will its members react to your message? Will they understand it as you mean it? Are there words or images that have particular significance for them? Think it through before you speak or act.

chapter three

Name_____ **Date**_____

1. You receive a phone call at your office from a reporter working at home. You have been concentrating on a project unrelated to the reporter's questions, and your co-workers have gone home for the day. In a short essay, describe the dynamics of this communication process and the potentials for interference.

2. Watch a TV newscast and observe any instances of physical interference. Write those down and then use your imagination to list additional physical interferences that could have occurred.

Name_____   **Date**_____

3. Listen to a radio newscast while driving in your car and observe any instances of physical interference during the process. (Try not to have an accident!) Write a short essay detailing how the interference affected your perception of the message.

4. Read the front page of a newspaper and all the jumps from those stories. Note all instances of environmental, mental, cultural, or emotional interference. Write an essay covering what you have learned about your own news filtering predispositions.

Chapter 4

Understanding the Media

Effective public relations practitioners have a thorough understanding of the media. That's the bottom line.

Consider this: How can you persuade the media to do what you want if you don't know what makes them tick? What buttons to push? What THEY want? The answer is obvious. You can't.

Therefore, your alternatives are to be an ineffective PR person—or to learn about the media.

Basics of General Psychology 101

Always keep in mind the Golden Rule: be nice. Reporters, editors, photographers and other media personnel are human beings with the same feelings and egos as everyone else.

Generally, members of the press are working under tremendous pressures: deadlines, the boss' demands, competition. The stress sometimes makes them cranky, as it would anyone else. If they're cranky with you, don't take it personally and don't respond in kind. That would be counterproductive.

How do you feel when someone complains about your work, especially when you've done the best you can under the circumstances? Do you feel defensive? Do you feel annoyed with the person complaining? Do you feel less inclined to do this person any favors? What makes you think members of the media are any different? Ergo, if a correction is in order for a giant error, handle it gently. A reporter who appears to be thick-skinned and aggressive probably also has a fragile ego. Be nice. Pick your spots for pointing out mistakes. Otherwise you can kiss your media relations goodbye.

Do you resent someone looking over your shoulder and nit-picking everything you do? Does it make you feel frustrated, especially if the person is uninformed or has a particular axe to grind? Members of the press are no different. Don't tell them how to do their jobs, or you'll lose your persuasive advantage. You can SUGGEST things, in a pleasant and non-aggressive manner. But don't pressure them or be overly critical.

Always behave professionally and wear your "I'm here to help you" hat when dealing with the media. "I'm on your side." "I understand what you need." If the roles were reversed, wouldn't you respond positively? Of course.

Occasionally you will encounter members of the press who are cynical and suspicious, who have lost their perspective, whose ethics are suspect, or who are out to make a name for themselves. You'll have to be alert for these personality disorders and handle each case individually, using your best judgment and persuasive skills to avoid damage to your organizations's image without alienating the reporter or editor in question. It can be a tricky situation, and you'll need to stop and think each time you make any statements to them.

When there's a big, visual event, local TV news organizations send out the microwave trucks en masse. Here they assemble for an address by President Clinton.
Photo by Merry Shelburne

News Judgment

A highly developed news judgment will serve you well as a PR specialist. What is news judgment? It is the ability to sense what is news and what is not news . . . what will be of interest to the general public and thus to the news media. It is the ability to have PERSPECTIVE and separate what is important to your organization from what is important to the press. It is the ability to discern the properties of an appealing feature or human interest story and the accompanying visual or photographic opportunities.

Reporters often are encouraged to do what are called trend stories and enterprise stories, and you need to be alert to those possibilities within your own company. An enterprise story is one that deals with a local example of a bigger national story, or is a further-investigated aspect of a previous story. A trend story is one that pulls together all the threads of an emerging fad, trend or cultural direction. By making thoughtful suggestions to editors, reporters and assignment editors, you can do them a favor and simultaneously enhance your own organization's image.

In short, you must put yourself in the shoes of the media and understand what they need. If, instead, you bombard them with trivial press releases and requests for hand-shaking photos, your company logo on an envelope soon will mean an automatic trip to the circular file. And then where will you be when you have something really big and newsworthy to publicize? Nowhere. The media will perceive you as an annoying person with no news judgment, and they will ignore your attempts to get their attention.

Despite your good news judgment, there will be uninformed people within your organization who pressure you to "put this in the paper;" and "this" frequently will be something non-newsworthy. That's where your high wire-walking nightmare begins, and that topic will be addressed fully in chapters 6 and 7.

The Print Media

National Newspapers

USA Today, the *Wall Street Journal* and the *Christian Science Monitor* are national newspapers. Stories are written at bureaus, then telecommunicated to the home office where they are composed onto pages. The pages are then sent via satellite to printing locations around the country, where the editions are published and distributed simultaneously. Getting coverage in one of these publications is difficult but not impossible. The best avenue is a media advisory to the local bureau chief or a regional wire service. Be sure to tailor your story idea to the needs of the paper: financial emphasis for the *WSJ,* more in-depth stories for the *CSM,* and short and punchy for *USA Today.*

Daily Newspapers

Most daily newspapers in the United States go to press in the wee hours of the morning, which means reporters and editors usually work afternoons and evenings. Some journalists work at home or on-site at an event and modem stories from their laptop computers via phone line to their publication's central computer.

Newspaper pages are created on computer screens in a process known as pagination. This is the front page of the *Daily News of Los Angeles* sports section. *Photo courtesy of the Daily News of Los Angeles*

Story ideas normally are generated by both editors and reporters during informal conversations or formal story meetings. Reporters usually have a "beat" or specific area to cover, such as crime, schools, city council, etc. Then of course there are specialists like movie critics, sports writers, and those who work for the business section. All of these reporters are supposed to be familiar with activities in their particular areas and frequently will suggest story ideas. Editors then give the okay, or suggest a different angle, or say "no", or table the idea in favor of something else. When a story is assigned, a length usually is assigned as well, and a deadline. The deadline can be later that day or next week.

Generally, with a large newspaper, all the editors meet in the early afternoon to discuss what's going where in that day's edition. If there's a late-breaking story—and frequently there is—everything can change at the last minute. But the editors want to at least have a plan in place. They plot what stories will go above the fold on page one, what art (photographs and illustrations) to run and where, what articles will jump to what page, etc. Then it's up to the reporters to investigate and write those stories, up to the photographers to take their photos, up to the "desk" to edit stories for errors and write headlines. And someone else will be designated to design the pages and prepare "dummies" (scaled-down models of pages indicating where each story goes).

Some small newspapers still computer-typeset their stories on long galleys of type which are waxed on the back, cut and pasted up on boards the size of actual pages. The pasteup people follow what's indicated on the dummies. However, desktop publishing systems are becoming more and more popular, and the technical quality of output devices (printers) is increasing rapidly. Most newspapers now use desktop and either employ computer scanners to digitally integrate the artwork or leave a space to pasteup half-tones (photographs need to be re-composed into a dot pattern so they will reproduce on the printing press).

Relatively inexpensive printers have been developed that can output an entire page, which eliminates the need for pasteup people. With such a device, editors can lay out a full page on the computer screen and simply push a button to print it out. Presto: no more X-acto knives, wax or pasteup boards.

Whether pages are produced by computer or pasted up, the next step is to photograph the pages on a machine called a stat camera. The resulting large negatives are used to make metal plates, which are then put on an offset printing press.

Technical issues aside, the successful PR practitioner knows reporters have NO CONTROL over placement of their stories or what the headlines say. And frequently they have no control over what they cover, what art runs with their articles or how many mistakes are made on the copy desk. Sometimes editors demand that reporters go back to their sources and ask more probing questions, or take a different or more sensational angle in the story. You need to know how the chain of command works and the personalities at each newspaper in your area.

You also need to know precisely what your local dailies NEED, and that depends on the size of the paper. The larger the newspaper, the less concerned editors are about local stories that would be of interest to only a few readers. You'll need to take that into consideration when deciding what information to dispense.

If you're seeking coverage by a large metropolitan daily, you'll have to come up with an angle that will interest a considerable segment of its readership—especially if you represent a small organization. Keep track of pop culture trends and events that are attracting lots of attention. When your company has a similar event or perhaps a specialist who can comment on a current issue, that's the time to approach the big papers. They'll be much more responsive. If you work for a larger regional or national organization, your chances for coverage are much better; but the same principle of relationship to current topics holds true.

Depending on the situation, you have the following choices: a news release, feature idea advisory, media alert, photo opportunity advisory, fax or phone call. These options are discussed thoroughly in Section II. The major thing you must keep in mind, however, is large dailies do NOT publish company news releases. Reporters and editors prefer to receive advisories or media alerts with several contact phone numbers. They want to write their own stories. And they do not appreciate follow-up calls inquiring about possible publication dates. If you don't make a habit of it, you may be able to get away with ONE non-pressure follow-up call asking if you can do anything to help them gather further information. That's it. If you pester them, you run the risk of damaging your relationship. You have to look at the big picture and consider what might happen down the road, so make the best presentation you can, and then let it go.

Most newspapers publish some sort of calendar of events. The larger the paper, the more segregated the calendars. As a PR specialist, you'll need to know precisely which calendar is best to publicize an upcoming event, what format each paper requires, the necessary lead time, and exactly which editor to contact. The more you follow their rules, the better chance you have of getting the publicity you seek.

A word about photographs: If you're offering a photo opportunity, make sure it's a good one with lots of possibilities. Take deadlines into consideration when you plan photo ops, and try to arrange proper lighting and good backgrounds. Have some suggestions ready for artistic angles and make sure you or your assistant are on-site to answer questions and provide proper spelling of names. Then, just be available to help the photographer. Don't get in the way. If YOU want to provide photos, remember large dailies want to take their own pictures, just like they want to write their own stories. An exception might be a photo accompanying a calendar item. Make it a black and white print or a color negative. Size is unimportant, since the paper will crop, enlarge or reduce when making the half-tone.

Smaller dailies are more anxious to cover local events, but they also have smaller, more inexperienced staffs with which to work. Sometimes they are grateful for a news release or a photo to help fill a page. If you represent a local company, you will have more contact with these reporters and editors than those at the metropolitan dailies. These journalists may be open to everything you throw at them, providing you have demonstrated good news judgment and followed the rules mentioned above.

Try to keep in mind newspapers survive on advertising revenue, and sometimes those ads squeeze out stories at the last minute. It's not the reporter's decision, and you shouldn't take it personally if your company's coverage bites the dust. The local news hole in most smaller dailies is 5 to 10 percent.

The Weeklies

Weekly newspapers generally are desperate for stories and photographs. Many times they do not have a reporter or photographer available, and you need to step in and help them. For instance, you could take pictures at an event and then hand over the roll of film to the paper's reporter. Usually these journalists are young and inexperienced, and they will rely on you to give them the important information. Do it. Area residents frequently read their local weeklies cover to cover, so it's in your organization's best interest to cooperate.

Occasionally small papers will try to pressure you to advertise in exchange for covering an event or printing your news releases. That would be unethical on their part and on yours, so steer clear of those situations. Just say No. And continue to send them stories.

Commentaries

Perhaps you have specialists or experts employed at your company whose opinions would be valuable to the reading public. If that's the case, don't miss the opportunity to submit opinion pieces to area newspapers. A byline by one of your organization's staffers is excellent free publicity—even if you have to ghost-write the article yourself with the person's permission. Newspapers always look for well-written pieces on a variety of topics and may even solicit them in a boxed notice on the editorial pages. Be sure to follow their rules when you submit the commentary, and don't pester the editorials editor if it isn't published.

In addition, frequently reporters like to call on experts to get their opinions about current events. You can submit a list of your company's specialists, their areas of expertise and their phone numbers to city editors—with a note offering assistance. This would be well-received, as long as you don't follow up with insistent phone calls.

News Services

If time does not permit contact with every newspaper, making use of news services ("wire" services) can be advantageous. Most papers, even weeklies, subscribe to some sort of regional or national service to supplement the work of their reporters and photographers. It's all handled with computers and satellite dishes, or perhaps microwave dishes with a local wire. There also are specialty news and feature services—catering to different kinds of publications—that would accept appropriate information from you. Nationally, Associated Press (which also has regional wires) is probably the best news service to use. The other U.S. national and regional wire, United Press International, has had its financial ups and downs. Reuters, based in England, has a large toe-hold in the U.S. and is utilized more and more frequently. And, depending on the type of company you represent, you might want to make use of regional PR newswires.

Respected PR specialists with good news judgment are successful in getting information out in this manner, and many local services depend on PR people for this data. If you have an upcoming newsworthy event, a timely feature idea or a photo opportunity, you might consider faxing concise information to the appropriate news services. They will get the word out in a short period of time. Do NOT send news releases to them.

Magazines

Magazines come in all sizes, shapes, colors and specialties. They publish weekly, bi-weekly, monthly and quarterly. They're national or regional. Most fall into one of the following categories: news, general interest, entertainment, special interest, or trade publication. Depending on the size and type of organization you represent, you could make use of these media outlets to enhance your company's image. But before you make contact, study the publication's content and audience to be sure they're appropriate. What are the magazine's policies? Do the editors want pre-packaged material or simply an advisory? Find out.

Trades

Many times trade publications are the best way to go because they reach almost everyone involved in your organization's industry. Small journals of this nature may require some advertising in return for the publicity, so be prepared for that contingency.

There also are BIG trades, like *Daily Variety,* that you would want to cultivate if you have clients in the entertainment industry.

Tabloids

The tabloids—those unprofessional, entertaining, useless, frequently ridiculous publications for sale near the check out counter—are to be avoided at all costs. They thrive on gossip, scandal, half-truths and even lies, and you must steer your organization away from them. There's very little they could do to enhance your company's image. Reporters, editors and photographers from these publications frequently have ethical lapses. They've lost many libel lawsuits but seem not to care because the courtroom drama just gives them more publicity. If you're approached by a representative from this type of operation—run.

There are, however, many quality newspapers printed tabloid size that should not be avoided. The *Wall Street Journal, Christian Science Monitor* and *L.A. Weekly* are three that come to mind immediately.

Advertising

Advertising in newspapers and magazines can be extremely expensive. The larger the publication's circulation, the larger your bill.

If you work for a big company, it may have a separate advertising department or hire outside advertsing firms. If that is the case, you may need to coordinate your PR efforts with the ad campaign. Or, it's possible you will not be involved at all.

Conversely, if you're employed by a smaller organization, you may handle advertising in your own department. There are those who consider advertising an offshoot of public relations. If advertising is one of your responsibilities, there are several things to consider:

1. Cost. What will your budget allow?

2. Goal. What do you want the ads to accomplish?

3. Target audience. Whom do you want to reach in order to accomplish those goals?

Section III of this book, "The PR Campaign," provides details about advertising procedures as part of an overall public relations effort.

The Broadcast Media

Television and radio offer more instantaneous regional and national coverage for your organization or company, and we're not talking about just the news. There are radio talk shows, cable TV network talk shows, network TV talk shows, regional TV infotainment shows, and even infomercials. The possibilities are endless, if your company has the bucks.

Network Television News

To get your organization coverage on national network TV news, first you have to understand what the producers are looking for. They want visual. They want relatively uncomplicated information that will interest their vast audience. They want an angle that relates to a major story or cultural trend or has appealing human interest value.

If you have a story idea that fits the criteria, your first step is to contact the network's closest bureau chief. You can reach this person late morning their time via news service, personal phone call, or a brief fax or media alert designed to pique interest. Do not send a news release or other in-depth information unless it is requested. Do not pester or harrangue. Maintain your professionalism. If the bureau chief doesn't take the bait, you can try corporate headquarters, which are in New York for ABC, CBS and NBC and in Atlanta for Cable News Network (CNN). The Fox network doesn't have a national newscast—yet. In any case, do not apply undue pressure.

For the time being, network newscasts typically air for a half-hour at 6:30 p.m. right after the local news. That has changed in the past and probably will change again as the networks scramble for advantages in the ratings. CNN, of course, is a 24-hour cable network where you can find news at any time.

A word about ratings: The A.C. Nielsen Co. conducts surveys to determine how many people are watching a particular show during the four ratings periods each year. (Arbitron conducts regional and local surveys for radio.) We won't get into details about the specifics of these polls, but the plain truth is they're not very accurate. Network executives know they're not accurate and advertising executives know they're not accurate, but nothing more accurate has been invented. Ergo, the ratings are used to determine how much the networks can charge advertisers for air time, and that's why ratings are so important to programming.

Conglomerates rule in the media business. This empty KTLA news set looks eerie on the occasion of the station's sale to Tribune.
Photo courtesy of the Daily News of Los Angeles

Local Television News

Most often you will be dealing with local TV newscasts, and there are four kinds: those at stations owned and operated by the networks, those at stations that are network affiliates, those at independent local stations and those at stations that are part of public broadcast television (PBS).

All of the assignment editors for these newscasts are looking for the same thing: visual, topical, relatively simple short stories. Are they looking for news? There's an old joke that it's not news unless a TV camera is present, and there's some truth to that. How often do you see a story without visuals? But mostly, except for PBS, they're looking for RATINGS. It's an unfortunate state of affairs, because a majority of Americans get their news from TV; and an informed electorate is imperative for a democracy to function. But we digress.

In a large market (metropolitan area) stories are gathered from a combination of sources: news services, newspapers, tips from informants, police and fire radio reports, other TV newscasts, beat reporters (just like the print media), radio newscasts, network satellite feeds, and, from public relations people, media alerts, press conferences and photo opportunities.

Half-hour newscasts typically run at 6 p.m. and 11 p.m., but many stations broadcast hour-long and half-hour news shows at noon, 4 and 5 p.m., 9 and 10 p.m., or for an hour at 6 p.m. It all depends on the market and the competition. You need to know when the news is broadcast at each station in your area.

The person who decides what will be covered is the assignment editor, who usually can be reached in the late morning. At large TV stations, there is a day assignment editor, a night assignment editor and a weekend assignment editor. There's also a traffic desk, which handles transportation for the crews. Smaller outfits have an assignment desk, which may or may not be occupied at any particular hour. The assignment editor decides which reporters and which camera crews will cover which events, and keeps a log of who is where. When a breaking story occurs, crews assigned to softer, more feature oriented events may be pulled off those and sent to the new location.

A typical news crew is a reporter, a camera person and a sound person. Sometimes a field producer comes along. The crew usually travels in a van, which may or may not be equipped with a microwave dish to broadcast live. In smaller towns, there may be just one news crew for a station.

On early weekday afternoons, usually the assignment editor, news editor, the producer (responsible for the show's content) and the director (responsible for the show's overall appearance) have a story meeting to determine how long each piece will be and in what order it will appear. This procedure emulates the way newspapers conduct business, and, as with newspapers, when there is a late-breaking story the whole plan can go down the drain. But at least a plan is in place. News crews already are out in the field or on their way, with more to be sent out at the direction of the assignment editor.

Typically, when a crew returns, the reporter bargains with the producer about the length of the "package". The producer wins the argument. Then the reporter retires to an editing room, with or without a tape-editing specialist, and prepares a package that will be aired during the newscast. Meanwhile, newswriters prepare the script, which contains words for the anchors to read from the TelePrompTer and directions for the engineer.

For the PR practitioner, news judgment is essential when trying to persuade TV news to give you some air time. Don't approach assignment editors unless you have something that fits their needs. If you're going to schedule a press conference, keep their deadlines in mind. Reporters usually need a minimum of an hour to prepare a package, and they prefer not to work in the early morning. Photo opportunities or press conferences between 11 a.m. and 2 p.m. are best.

If you want reporters to cover an upcoming event, do not give assignment editors more than a week's or less than two day's advance notice. If it's for the weekend, be sure to contact the weekend assignment editor. A media alert or fax advisory should do the trick, with emphasis on the best time to arrive, exact location, parking, visual and audio opportunities, the main aspect of the event and contact names and numbers. If you're short on time, direct your communique to a news service.

For a feature idea, use a similar process. Briefly outline on a media advisory sheet the feature opportunity, why it would make a good piece, and list contact names and numbers. Also ask if the assignment editor would like additional, more detailed information. He or she will appreciate your courtesy for not sending a thick packet.

When dealing with a PBS station, remember those news executives are far more interested in longer, in-depth packages. Some PBS organizations do not initiate newscasts at all and rely instead on national shows such as the *Lehrer Report*. Unless a news operation is based near your company, you'll probably have to deal with a national syndicated show. In that case, contact the producer by mail or fax, or, if time is short, by phone. Again, be sure what you have to offer is timely, worthwhile and of interest to the PBS audience.

Caution: even if an assignment editor indicates a crew will be present, there's a chance that crew won't show up. Unless your press conference, photo op or event is of major importance, your scheduled crew could be pulled off that assignment if a big story breaks. And, of course, you may get no response at all to your advisory. If either of these things happen, don't be disillusioned and don't take it personally.

When a TV news crew arrives at your workplace, whether it's a surprise or not, it's your job to be helpful and cooperative. That means facilitating a good place for the van to park, having information at your fingertips, finding key personnel to be interviewed if requested, directing or escorting the camera crew to the appropriate location and in general trying to make the whole operation run smoother. Those are the things TV reporters expect from a PR professional. If you're running a press conference, be mindful of the backdrop, make sure the audio system is working, see to it that your speakers are dressed appropriately (avoid stripes, all black or white), and provide enough space and light.

Always keep in mind that newscasts are looking for short audio/visual sound bites (also known as actualities) of 20- to 30-second duration. If you or your company rep have something to say, try to pre-plan your words to fit into those parameters. Be precise, keep it simple, and don't hem and haw.

Talk, Infotainment & Tabloids

TV is exploding with local and national talk shows like *Larry King Live,* interview programs such as *Meet the Press,* investigate reporting ventures in the *60 Minutes* realm, tawdry tabloid shows like *Hard Copy,* morning news/talk forums such as *Today,* and reality-based programs like *Cops.*

Some of these increasingly popular shows provide possibilities for enhancing the image of your organization. Talk shows, interview programs and news/talk forums require a continuous lineup of new guests, especially at the local level. Producers constantly seek interesting, poised, articulate people to populate their shows.

Put your TV remote on scan and look for programs whose formats seem appropriate for a guest appearance by your company's representatives. Contact the producers by mail and follow up a few days later with one friendly phone call. Send them a short, concise fact sheet offering experts on topical subjects, new products, new trends, etc. Unless you represent a well-known organization or can offer something truly astounding, stick to the local shows. As with the other media, give your best effort and then let it go if there is no response.

Advertising

The price for advertising on television, with the exception of local cable, is astronomical. If your company is large enough to afford regular TV advertising, chances are the PR department will not be responsible for this task. However, local cable operators offer minimal rates, and with a small budget you can produce and air a 30-second commercial on the likes of CNN, MTV, ESPN, USA, etc. in your area.

Again, pay attention to your goal and what target audience can help you reach that goal. Then tailor the commercial to those people and air it on the cable channels that attract those viewers.

Radio

Like their counterparts on TV, radio reporters need short sound bites to air live or put on tape for later editing. You or your company representative need to prepare a concise, simple statement and deliver it with no "uhs" or "ers." Be polite, professional and truthful. The average person takes about 10 seconds to say 25 words or 20 seconds to say 50, so keep that in mind if you have time to prepare.

Local

Most radio stations are local and carry local news programming or "rip 'n' read" news updates. Rip 'n' read refers to radio wire copy "ripped" off the computer and read immediately over the air. Many major markets have at least one all-news station, and if that is the case in your area you'll need to become familiar with the program directors' needs.

Use your good news judgment to determine if an upcoming event is worthy of radio coverage. If you have an all-news station in your area, be sure to communicate directly with the program director via a media advisory no more than a week ahead or less than two days before the event. If no station in your area has its own reporters, don't expect radio coverage by DJs.

National

National Public Radio (NPR) and the Mutual Broadcasting System basically are the only country-wide networks. If your event or whatever is of national interest, contact the program director by mail and follow up with one call. Associated Press and the three major TV networks all have broadcast wires, and the best way to reach them is by mail or fax to the regional bureau. In some instances where time is short, you may want to contact them by phone.

Talk Shows

Radio talk shows are one of the fastest growing phenomena in the country, and these programs have huge audiences. As we recommended for TV talk shows, give the dial a spin and find a format that's appropriate for your organization. Then contact the producer by mail and follow up with one call.

Advertising

Radio advertising is expensive, especially during drive time (early morning and late afternoon). If your budget allows placing these types of commercials, choose the stations carefully. Again, decide which target audience will help you achieve your goal, and to what stations this audience listens. Then prepare an ad that will appeal to those people.

Public Service Announcements

The Federal Communications Commission requires licensed broadcasters to devote a portion of their air time, for free, to public service announcements. If you work for a non-profit organization or a company that is sponsoring a legitimate charity fundraiser, you can make use of PSAs. Normally these are 10-, 20-or 30-second spots submitted in writing directly to each station's public service director. Most stations require several weeks' lead time to put the PSA into rotation to be read by the announcers. They also need the PSA presented in a particular format, which varies from area to area. In addition, some stations accept pre-taped PSAs that adhere to their technical guidelines.

Conglomerates

Be aware that conglomerates rule in the media. Here's an example from the sports world: Time Warner bought CNN from Ted Turner, and TW also owns *Sports Illustrated*. Now we have the CNNSI website. ESPN was purchased by Disney, which also owns ABC. Media mogul Rupert Murdock has launched FOX Sports Net to compete with ESPN,

Case Study

Here's a situation where a true understanding of the media saved the college a lot of grief:

It was the middle of the summer session when I got a call from a newspaper reporter asking about a complaint a young woman was making. According to her, the college's TV production class was producing a pornographic movie.

My reaction: "WHAT???!!!"

I said I'd call him right back as soon as I found out what was happening. Immediately I contacted the teacher of that class, who is a good friend of mine. The instructor had heard about the complaint that morning, had investigated, and was about to call me. Of course, he had been in touch with the appropriate members of the college administration, who were in an uproar.

Here's what had happened: Students in that class were required to submit a script to the teacher before beginning production on their individual short movies. One student—we'll call him Bob—submitted a script and it was approved. Then he hooked up with some outside producer, and, using college equipment, began taping an entirely different script . . . without the knowledge of the teacher, of course. Bob and his producer actually did a casting call and got responses from aspiring actresses—including the young woman

who was complaining. She was protesting a scene where she briefly would be (gulp!) topless.

Needless to say, the instructor recovered the video equipment and gave Bob an F.

As soon as I had been briefed, I got back to the reporter and filled him in on the situation. I was completely honest. Then, I called his competition—the two other papers that regularly cover the college—and told those editors the whole story. As it turns out, the complaining woman and her boyfriend were making the rounds of all the media outlets they could find, and reporters at both papers had been about to call me. The fact that I called them first made the college look really good. We were being totally upfront, so obviously we had nothing to hide.

I continued to update the reporters by phone with each new development—saving them the trouble of actually coming to the campus. All of them thanked me many times for that and for being so straightforward.

The college was front page news for three days, but the stories were fair and well-balanced. Eventually the reporters began to believe the young woman and her boyfriend were simply seeking publicity, and the stories stopped. If we hadn't been so cooperative, the media probably would have dragged us through the mud for weeks.

Related Web Sites

www.cnn.com
www.nytimes.com
www.cbs.com
www.msnbc.com
www.WashingtonPost.com

and both have web sites . . . as do CBS and NBC sports. Ergo, broadcast networks, cable networks, and the internet are combining to give YOU even more opportunities for well-placed PR efforts.

Conclusion

Now that you understand how the media works, you're ready to begin educating your workmates—especially those who might come into contact with the press. You're also ready to learn the specifics of dealing with journalists. Read on.

chapter four

Name_____ **Date**_____

1. You're the new PR/advertising specialist for a huge poultry farm (1000 employees) located near a town of 20,000 and about 20 miles from a city of 200,000. The small town has a newspaper published twice a week. The city has one daily newspaper, 4 music radio stations, 1 talk/music radio station and 1 all-news radio station. The city also has 3 TV network affiliate stations and 2 independent TV stations. One cable operator serves both city and town residents. In the city there is an AP regional bureau and an independent metro wire news service. And the city's Chamber of Commerce has a monthly magazine/newsletter.

    For the 4th of July, your company is sponsoring a Jubilee—picnic, small fair and softball tournament—with a $5 per person admission fee. All proceeds will go to build a new baseball field for the local high school. You have a $200 budget to promote the event. Which media outlets would be interested in this story, and how would you approach each of them? Write a short essay.

Name_____ **Date**_____

2. Make an appointment to tour a local newspaper on deadline. Watch (but don't get in the way) and take notes for a couple of hours, then write a short essay about what you observed and learned.

3. Contact the public relations department at a TV station, explain you're a student, and ask permission to visit and observe as many of the following operations as possible: the news room, the studio during a newscast, the control room during a newscast, an editing bay, or out in the field with a camera crew. Write a short essay describing what you learned.

Name_____ **Date**_____

4. Call a newspaper or magazine photo editor and make arrangements to spend some time out in the field with a photojournalist. Observe, then write a short essay describing your experiences. If possible, take along your own camera—then compare your shots with those published.

5. If there's a talk radio station or show in your vicinity, call and ask permission to visit the studio during a broadcast. Interview the person who books the guests and find out what qualities he/she prefers in a publicist. What makes that person say "Yes!" when approached by a PR professional? Compose a list of likes (successful strategies) and dislikes (unsuccessful strategies) from that person's perspective. Bring the list to class for discussion.

Name_____ **Date** _____

6. In a major metropolitan area, with two major daily papers and seven TV stations, which of the following stories is newsworthy enough for you to alert the media? Show your news judgment by ranking them in order of importance. Be prepared to defend your choices during a class discussion.

> Your organization is holding a bake sale for a scholarship program.
> The VP has been caught embezzling company funds.
> A staff scientist has inadvertently invented bark-flavored chewing gum.
> The CEO's daughter announces her engagement.
> Your company's child care center has landed a federal grant.

7. The local newspaper has misspelled your new CEO's name throughout a story announcing his/her appointment. Write a short essay about how you would handle that situation.

Name_____ **Date** _____

8. Which stories are most appropriate for which media? Be prepared to defend your choices during a class discussion.

__ Wedding announcement   A. Trades
__ Fire captain hand-makes teddy bears for kids   B. Metro Daily
__ Client lands spot on daytime soap   C. Network News
__ Company's free picnic for tornado survivors   D. Local Weekly
__ Expert's opinion on war in Angola   E. Radio Talk Show
__ Client has new book   F. Local TV News

9. You have a small budget to promote an upcoming event that will appeal to teenagers. Where do you spend your advertising dollars, and why? Write a short essay.

Chapter 5

Developing Credibility with the Media and Your Bosses

A public relations practitioner cannot operate in a vacuum. Your knowledge and skills will do you no good unless you have established credibility with both the media and your bosses. But to do that, first you'll probably have to prove yourself.

Bosses and Co-Workers

Unlike computer programming or some other technical field, public relations is one of those areas on which almost everyone feels free to comment. You will encounter those who believe PR takes no skills or training. You will encounter those who see no reason for employing a PR specialist. You will encounter those who think the media exist simply to publicize your organization's events or that the media are to be avoided at all costs.

In short, you will encounter co-workers who believe they know everything, when actually they know absolutely nothing about the art of public relations. Your natural inclination will be to shout, "You have no idea what you're talking about!" But of course you can't do that . . . at least not until you've established your credibility.

The fact that you're occupying a position in a public relations office or have been hired by a client indicates at least your company acknowledges the need for a PR specialist. But before your bosses can trust you, they'll have to see what you can do. And they'll have to be trained, which is covered in Chapter 6.

In a typical catch-22, to prove your effectiveness to your bosses, first you'll have to build a relationship with the media. And that is difficult to do if your bosses are interfering by maintaining contact with journalists. Ergo, the number one priority is to convince management and co-workers to cease all communication with reporters for a period of time.

Then go to work on the media. The specifics are discussed below, but once you've established your credibility with the press you can persuade journalists to give your organization some positive publicity. Don't attempt a complicated campaign—just one or two simple items. When your efforts succeed, you'll have proof of your effectiveness to lay on the table.

It also helps to sit down with management and explain the benefits of having a company spokesperson. Use your persuasive communication skills and don't shy away from a little razzle-dazzle. Tell them what you can accomplish and the burdens you can lift from their shoulders. Put it in writing. Use graphic flow charts. Show them your success stories. Look them in the eye and make sure they understand. Convince them to let you (and your staff, if you have one) handle everything without interference.

If you're lucky, you may discover your bosses are not "PR-impaired" and that they understand most of the concept. That will make your job much easier, especially if you have a CEO or client who instinctively knows what to say to reporters.

The Media

Step one in establishing your credibility with the press is to research what media cover your organization on a regular basis and the names of specific reporters or editors.

Next, place a phone call to each of these people. Introduce yourself briefly and courteously and ask if you can drop by their place of business for a quick visit. It's important they can put a face with your name. Be sure to ask what is a CONVENIENT time for them. Then, be on time. Shake hands and smile. Tell them who you are and that you will be contacting them with legitimate news advisories when they're warranted. Give them a business card or calling card with your office and HOME phone numbers and tell them you're always available. Invite them to visit your office at any time. Then, since they're probably quite busy, make a quick departure.

Individual contact is preferable to a group meeting with strangers because unknown variables or sudden personality conflicts can interfere with communication when more than two people are involved. In addition, some reporters might be resentful if they are "summoned" to your office. Therefore, go to them for the initial contact. Impress them with your knowledge of what is needed to make their jobs easier and your awareness of how busy they are. Keep it brief.

If there are news or wire services in your area, get the phone and fax numbers of the "budget desks." Then fax an introduction, with your name, company, position, office phone and home phone. Make it clear you always are available for their calls, and ask that this advisory be posted or filed with other sources.

When you make your second contact, reporters will feel they know you, and that is much easier than a sudden introduction under deadline pressure.

Now show them your good news judgment. A few days after you meet, mail or fax a media advisory about a truly newsworthy event, or a clever feature idea tied into a current issue, or a colorful and lively photo opportunity, etc. Do NOT send a news release to large newspapers, the broadcast media or news services.

If there is a small newspaper covering your organization, send a well-written news release composed in professional journalistic style, or a media alert offering to supply photos or other information. Chapters 10, 11 and 12 of this book cover in detail the various media contact devices.

Then wait. You should get some press reaction, depending on the importance and timeliness of the advisory's subject matter. It would be unusual to get no feedback; but if that happens, don't despair. Do NOT call reporters or editors and ask why they're not responding. That definitely would cause you to get off on the wrong foot in your new relationship. Just try again the next time. Perhaps your news judgment was misguided, or perhaps it was a heavy news day and you'll hear from the media later.

Keep sending out advisories whenever they're warranted. Contact individual reporters and editors and ask how you can make their jobs easier. What kinds of leads would they like from you? What types of specific stories or angles? Always make it clear you understand what is news and what isn't and that you won't be sending them inconsequential advisories.

When journalists call you with questions, always be friendly and straightforward. If you don't know the answers, say so. Tell them you'll find out and then get back to them directly. Never leave a reporter hanging. If you can't get the information they seek right away, call them back and tell them you're working on it.

A metropolitan newspaper newsroom looks nothing like the typewriter- and paper-strewn office with wooden desks once common across the country. Today it's a mass of computer terminals, steel desks and TV sets. But one thing hasn't changed. Deadline pressures usually result in somewhat untidy work areas. *Photo courtesy of the Daily News of Los Angeles.*

Never, never, never lie to the media. Eventually they will discover the truth; and if you lied, nothing will derail your credibility faster. If reporters believe they cannot trust you, that you have no integrity, then your effectiveness is dead. You will not be able to persuade them to do anything, and when something happens that has image-damaging potential for your company, the press will show no mercy.

Avoid using "off the record" because journalists may be able to obtain the information elsewhere, and that might put a strain on your relationship. Never tell a reporter something and then afterwards say it was off the record. In fact, never tell a reporter anything you don't want to read in the newspapers or see on TV. If you don't want it reported, don't say it.

In extreme circumstances with a journalist you trust, you might say, for instance, "I can explain the whole thing to you off the record—if you'll accept those terms—and then I'm sure you'll agree it's not a story worth pursuing. It would be illegal for me to comment on the record because it's a legal matter."

Avoid the stoic "No comment." This is off-putting to both the media and the public and makes you and your organization look like you have something to hide. If you legally cannot comment on something, say WHY. EXPLAIN. Cite the specific law.

Always be friendly, helpful, straightforward and professional. Be mindful of the media's deadlines and reporters' egos. After awhile, the press will begin to trust you and appreciate your integrity, and that image of you should transfer to your organization.

Both

You'll have more to overcome if previous relationships between your company and the media have been strained. Journalists eventually may trust you but still distrust, for example, your CEO. In that case, the need for training or retraining your bosses and co-workers becomes imperative, and that process is discussed in detail in the next chapter.

Case Study

Reporters come and go, so the PIO has to keep re-establishing credibility with each new journalist. We invite them to campus, if they're interested, or we send them packets of information to make their jobs easier. They soon learn we're user-friendly.

GCC is a pleasant place to work, so there's not a lot of turnover in the college's administration; but occasionally there's a new vice president or dean, or a new member of the Board of Trustees. Just in case questions arise, we keep copies of every newspaper article that mentions the college. We utilize a clipping service, plus we clip the local paper ourselves. We then copy and reduce the stories onto 8-1/2 x 14 sheets. (Newsprint yellows, so the originals are discarded.)

By the end of each year, the collection is impressive. In fact, just one month is impressive. If any new person is foolish enough to suggest the college isn't getting any coverage, we just whip out that file and watch the eyes widen and the mouth drop open.

The clips file also is useful when faculty members want copies of stories concerning them (we send those out automatically), and when the PIO of the state organization of community colleges is publishing a book of articles.

In short, we take our clips file seriously. It's hard proof of the PIO's credibility. And when the technology becomes available to us, we will scan them into some sort of computer file for posterity.

Related Web Sites

saatchibuscomm.com
www.burrelles.inter.net
www.villagevoice.com/laweekly
www.usatoday.com

www

In any case, once you have established your credibility with both your boss and the media, it's time to call off the temporary ban on co-workers' communication with the press. But before you do that, institute the training program.

The PR Firm

If you work at a public relations firm, you will need to develop and maintain credibility with the media as described above. This is a much easier situation, however, because you won't have to intervene and cut off your bosses' access to reporters. Nor will you have to train your co-workers.

However, if you ARE one of the bosses of a PR company, make sure all your employees understand the basics we discuss in this book. If a staff member develops an adversarial relationship with one or more reporters, that will affect your firm's reputation with the media.

EXERCISES

Name_____ **Date**_____

1. A small local daily in your area has just hired a new, fresh-out-of-J-school reporter to cover subjects that encompass your organization. Write a short essay about what you should do to establish a good working relationship with that journalist.

2. You're new on the job. You've convinced your bosses to channel all media contact through you for awhile, and they've announced the new policy to your co-workers. Nevertheless, a middle-management type has called a reporter and complained about a story that was uncomplimentary to his/her department. Write a short essay about how you should handle the situation.

Name_____ **Date**_____

3. You own a small PR company and one of your employees calls an editor, on behalf of a client, to complain about a story. The editor angrily calls you. The employee has otherwise been doing a good job. Write a short essay about how you should handle the situation.

4. To establish your credibility with a local TV assignment editor, you choose a story you think is definitely newsworthy and fax him/her an alert. There is no response. What do you do next?

5. You've been working for a PR firm and now you've been hired by the city to fill the new position of PR director. The city has been treated poorly in the local daily newspaper. What are the major components of the strategy you should employ to rectify the situation?

Chapter **6**

Training Your Bosses and Co-workers

As has been stated in previous chapters, training your bosses and co-workers is critical to the successful practice of public relations. If you don't educate them, they could interfere in a situation and possibly cause harm to your organization's image as well as your own.

First—The Boss or Client

If you're really lucky, you might have a boss or client who already understands the subtleties of public relations. But even if he or she is leaning in that direction, it's best to make sure.

Depending on the organization of your company and the degree of its employees' sophistication, you should call a meeting or even set up a seminar with your CEO and the top brass. They may resist, but it's vital you educate them about the media and how to interact with members of the Fourth Estate.

The methodology for imparting your wisdom will vary with the circumstances, and you'll have to use your best judgment. It could be all you'll need is a quick meeting with your client or CEO to touch base. At the other extreme, if the top brass is hopelessly out of touch you'll have to insist on a day-long seminar.

In any case, there are certain points you must make sure they understand:

1. The media are privately-owned businesses that do NOT exist to provide publicity for your organization and do NOT "owe" your organization any favors.

2. Reporters operate on deadlines and cover stories assigned by their editors, who make those decisions based on their news judgment. Give your audience (seminar attendees) specific details about the deadlines of your local media.

3. Journalists usually have little control over placement of stories, headlines, photos, introductions to their TV reports or the length or emphasis of those reports. Their editors, copy editors, assignment editors and producers make those decisions.

4. The PR staff cannot guarantee to "put this in the paper" or "get this on the air" unless advertising space or air time is PURCHASED. You can only ATTEMPT to PERSUADE the editors.

5. It is not the media's job to present your company in a favorable light. It is the media's job to report in a truthful and fair manner, which means giving both or all sides of the story. If the coverage is less than favorable, perhaps it is deserved. However, if the story is false or unfair, then it is YOUR job, as the PR specialist, to make a decision. Is this incident sufficiently important to try convincing reporters and editors to make a correction? Is it worth risking your company's good relationship with the media? If so, then only YOU should make that contact, using all your tactful skills.

KNBC news team interviews designated spokesperson.
Photo by Susan Cisco

6. The company should have one spokesperson to deal with the press because that eliminates the probability of releasing conflicting information or even the possibility of a reporter playing one employee against another. United we stand, divided we fall. There may be exceptions, depending on your organization's complexity (see "Designated Spokesperson"). All official media contact initiated by your company should be accomplished exclusively through the PR office.

7. If the PR specialist is to interact effectively with the media, that person must be privy to all administrative decisions and discussions—in order to be prepared with damage control contingency plans. In fact, a little prior notice can prevent a fire instead of forcing the PR person to run around trying to put out the flames. And if an incident occurs that is potentially damaging, the PR office must be notified IMMEDIATELY.

8. Reporters and editors are human beings with feelings and egos like everyone else. Ergo, making nasty remarks to these people or trying to tell them how to do their jobs probably will have the opposite of the desired result. Anger and resentment may affect a journalist's attempt to be objective. Conversely, an occasional sincere word of praise or encouragement may have the subtle effect of enhancing your company's image in the reporter's eyes.

9. If someone other than, or in addition to, you will be an organizational spokesperson, some specific skill training is in order. Encourage them to:

Spokesperson Guidelines

A. Try to be prepared with a few succinct, precise words whenever a newsworthy (good or bad) situation arises.
B. Be brief.
C. Do not supply unrequested information in a tense situation.
D. Avoid long pauses or hems and haws.
E. Look reporters or cameras in the eye.
F. Tell the truth.
G. If a camera appearance is pre-arranged, wear appropriate clothing in good taste.
H. Do not use "off the record."
I. Avoid "no comment."
J. Do not say anything you don't want to see in the newspaper or hear on the radio or TV.

During the seminar, develop several scenarios and have the spokespersons react as if they were facing the media.

10. An official policy must be set for dealing with the media—detailing all employees' duties—including a disaster-preparedness plan for a natural or image-damaging disaster.

Now that the VIPs have been educated about the media, you should suggest an inter-office memo be circulated to all workers. If you're employed by a political campaign, this is doubly important. If a single client has family members who might come into contact with the press, they also would need educating.

Then—The Co-Workers

First of all, it's extremely important to establish that all employees are free to talk to the media at any time—as long as those not designated as official spokespersons (see below) do not represent themselves to reporters as official spokespersons. In other words, these employees would be giving their personal impressions and opinions and speaking as private citizens.

The First Amendment guarantees free speech, and attempts to restrict that freedom will only backfire. Employees will become resentful and disgruntled, and the media will get the impression your organization is hiding something by muzzling workers.

So make it absolutely clear to employees and to the press that there are no restrictions on free speech.

However, employees definitely are NOT REQUIRED to talk to the media if they feel uncomfortable. Instead, they should be encouraged to refer journalists to the organization's PR specialist or to other designated spokespersons.

In addition, employees should be encouraged to report to the PR office any incident, event, personal achievement, etc. that is potentially newsworthy.

The Designated Spokesperson

The number one spokesperson should be YOU—the PR expert. However, sometimes a company is so large and so diverse that one person can't possibly know detailed information about everything. Also, there are times when the media relations specialist or PR staff is not available. In those cases, designated spokespersons should be appointed to represent different departments within the organization, and that list should be circulated to every employee for reference. These spokespersons must be TRAINED by the PR expert.

Review

A memo should be distributed company-wide that includes some appropriate version of the following media communication policy:

Sample Media Communication Policy

1. Employees are free, but not required, to speak to the media at any time.
2. Certain employees have been designated as official company spokespersons.
   a. Please keep the attached list of spokespersons and their areas of expertise.
   b. Reporters seeking OFFICIAL comment should be referred to the appropriate person on the list.
3. Employees not designated as official spokespersons may NOT represent themselves to journalists as official spokespersons.
4. Appropriate (and polite) responses to reporters' questions should fall into one of these categories:

   ### Appropriate Staff Responses

   A. I'd be happy to tell you what I think personally, as long as you understand my comments do not necessarily represent the organization's official viewpoint.
   B. I'd prefer not to speak with you.
   C. I don't know the answer to your question, but you can get that information from _____.

5. Official media contact INITIATED by the company will be accomplished exclusively through the public relations office.
6. Employees are encouraged to report to the PR office any newsworthy personal achievement or upcoming event that would be of interest to the public. The PR office, supervised by Kelly Smith, is located at _____, extension _____.

Figure 6.1
Sample company guidelines booklet

Case Study

"Successful Media Relations: It's Everybody's Business!" is the title of the workshop I gave for administrators, faculty and staff. It was so well-received and I got so much positive feedback I decided to offer the seminar annually.

The flyer promoting the workshop announced, "Learn how to: Talk to Reporters...the good ones and the (dare we say it?) bad; Handle an image-damaging disaster; Participate in successful sound bites; Register complaints; Decide if you're official or unofficial; Publicize yourself and your events; Improve media relations to positively influence the college's image. Be prepared to participate."

When the audience members were assembled, I began by diagramming the process by which their own personal jobs depended on the college's good image. That really got their attention.

As I do in the journalism classes I teach, I used humor, role-playing, visual demonstrations and a great deal of audience participation to get across the points I wanted to make. The only downside was that a few people who really needed to be there (designated spokespersons with no clue) weren't there. I'll get them next time.

Related Web Sites

www.excite.com
index.opentext.net
www.iglou.com
www.mm-c.com

chapter six
EXERCISES

Name_____ **Date**_____

1. You've just been hired to handle the media in a city council person's re-election campaign in a major metropolitan area. You must deal with the candidate, a campaign manager, an advertising manager, your assistant, 15 general staffers, numerous volunteers, and the candidate's very vocal spouse. Write a short essay about how you should organize them for effective media relations.

Name_____ **Date** _____

2. Design a communique encouraging employees to report to you all newsworthy personal achievements and upcoming events that would be of interest to the public. Assume it's a large company with many departments.

Name_____   **Date**_____

3. Your organization has just hired a new boss who never tells you what's going on. Write a short essay explaining how you should handle the situation.

4. What components should be included in a company's media relations guidelines booklet? Do a sample mock-up and be prepared to discuss it in class.

Chapter 7

Walking the HighWire

Most of the time the practice of public relations resembles a high wire act, and if you fall off there might not be a net to catch you. Your organization or client is shoving you off balance on one side, and the media are pushing back from the other direction.

All you can do is keep walking the tightrope that stretches out to the horizon . . . and try not to slip.

Most of the pushing and shoving originates in a lack of understanding. Your company's bosses and employees do not understand the media, and journalists do not comprehend "civilians." YOU must keep the two sides, and yourself, in balance. That's why it's so important to educate the members of your organization and establish yourself as a buffer between the press and your client.

Egocentrism

Egocentrism is a condition affecting almost everybody at one time or another. It means self-centeredness. It means believing you or your department or your company is the most important entity in the world. It means lack of perspective. And, invariably, it leads to friction.

The PR specialist will encounter CEOs, clerks, reporters and editors who suffer from this condition—on both sides of the high wire. TACT is the key to achieving balance.

Co-worker: "Why didn't you put MY promotion in the paper? I want all my friends to know about it."

Reporter: "Can't you keep that guy off MY back? He's called twice and asked me to put his promotion on the front page. It's not news and I don't have time for this."

You: "Aaaaarrrgh!"

If this example sounds bizarre to you, think again. It's not that uncommon. Even if you have educated your co-workers about the media, an outbreak of egocentrism can still occur and destabilize your high wire.

What should you do in the case cited above? First, apologize to the reporter. Assure him/her YOU know a promotion from custodian to head custodian is not big news in a town of 200,000, and that's why you haven't sent out a news release about it. Tell the journalist you've been waiting for several months' worth of promotions to accumulate, and then you'll write a small release with all the company's appointments together. Cluck and soothe. Say you'll make sure the guy doesn't call again.

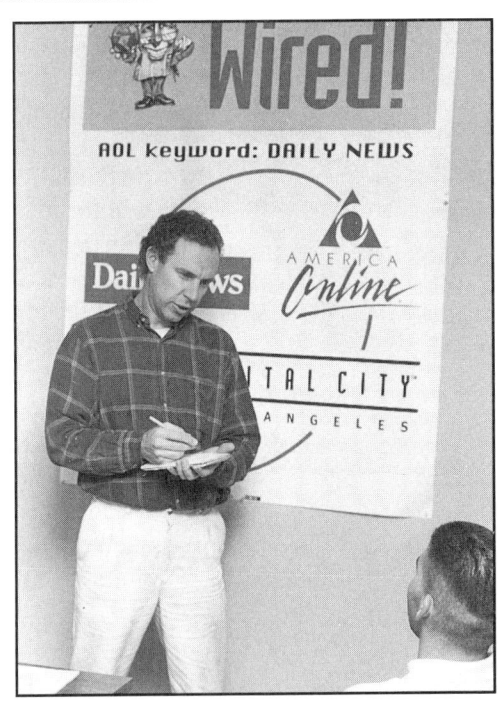

Daily News Los Angeles reporter Eric Noland concentrates on taking accurate notes during an interview. *Photo courtesy of the Daily News of Los Angeles*

Then, personally visit the employee in question. Cluck and soothe. Tell him YOU know he's important, but the local daily's policy is to print group rather than individual promotion stories. So, if he'll be just a little patient, the editor might be more inclined to run an article soon that mentions all the company's latest appointments. Gently remind him that pressuring reporters can be counterproductive, and review with him your organization's media communication policy. If you haven't already done so, offer to circulate company-wide a congratulatory flyer or to put the good news in an in-house publication.

Does the above exchange seem somewhat . . . political? Perhaps. But if you encounter a similar situation, you'll quickly have to concoct an equitable solution (a group promotion story in this case) and then try to convice both parties to go along with it. Maybe then your tightrope will stop wobbling—at least for awhile. You've soothed both sides and gained some positive PR for your company, using logic and persuasion, and that's OK.

Relations Gone Awry

Suppose a local TV reporter is trying to make a name for herself so she can move up from a small station to a network affiliate? Suppose she's looking under every rock for the slightest hint of impropriety by your organization? And suppose you're the Public Information Officer for that organization—the 80-member police department? The chief, unbeknownst to you, has circulated a memo criticizing the reporter and telling officers not to speak to her, and the reporter has obtained a copy of that memo. She calls you and threatens to read the note on the air.

You: "Aaaaarrrgh!"

Here's the dilemma. You want to protect the department's image (it deserves a good image) and you also want to maintain good media relations, but those two goals seem mutually exclusive. What to do?

First, tell the reporter the truth—that you knew nothing about the memo. Say you want to investigate the matter and you'll get right back to her.

Then, have a little chat with the chief and remind him (assuming you've already "educated" him) how important media relations are to the department. Gently suggest that he NEVER, EVER put that kind of message into a written memo again. Once it's in writing, it can't be taken back. Tell him you'll handle the situation and keep him apprised of your progress, and suggest he rescind (verbally!) his orders.

Next, call the reporter back. Make sure no more than a half hour has passed since she phoned you. As tactfully as possible, tell her the chief is unfamiliar with journalism and didn't realize she was just doing her job as a good investigative reporter. Say he didn't understand why she was so persistent when he knew his department was squeeky clean; and since you've explained it to him, he now believes she was just a little overenthusiastic. Invite her to come over and speak with whomever wants to talk to her, and stress that the department has absolutely nothing to hide. It is, after all, a public institution. Tell her you think she's doing a good job and anything else that will soothe her feelings. Don't lay it on too thick, but be sincere. That should put out the fire for the moment.

Finally, perhaps the next day, find an excuse to engage her boss in a casual conversation. Mention his reporter's enthusiasm and good investigative instincts. Chuckle and tell him it's too bad her talents are wasted in a small town, looking into the cleanest police department east of the Rockies. Bring up the chief's memo with a smile. Joke about sensationalistic big city newscasts and how their credibility suffers. Hopefully he'll get the point without getting his feathers ruffled, and he'll keep a closer eye on his reporter in the future.

Walking the HighWire.

The Nightmare

There may be times when a client, the politician for whom you work or a company employee does something dishonest or truly distasteful. Your advice will be to admit the truth before the media drag your client through the mud. But there might be legal considerations, or the person might refuse and then try to cover up the incident. If it's a given your allegiance is to the people who write your paycheck, then you must make some uncomfortable decisions. How much is your personal integrity worth to you?

The alternatives are fairly simple: you can quit and keep the reasons to yourself, you can "out" the boss and lose your job, you can stay out of the melee and become ineffective as a spokesperson (and probably be fired), or you can lie to the press and go down with the ship.

If you quit, your conscience will be clear but you might find yourself in line for unemployment checks for awhile. If you go to the press with the story and get fired, reporters will respect you but other employers might be skeptical about hiring you. If you waffle and do nothing, the result could be no job and no respect . . . but at least you'd know you didn't lie. If you take the last route and cover for your boss, forget about ever having any credibility with the media. The decision is yours.

The ideal, of course, is for the top brass to agree honesty is the best policy. That will allow you to function from the DAMAGE-CONTROL position; and if you've previously established a good working relationship with the media, they probably will give your organization the benefit of the doubt. It's bad enough when an employee does something that damages your company's image (and the public WILL find out eventually, whether you're up-front or not). But if the press suspects a cover-up and also casts doubt on the entire organization, that is much worse.

Overview

Walking the high wire is at once the most fearsome and most exhilarating aspect of public relations. It definitely is the biggest challenge, requiring equal parts of imagination, quick thinking, psychoanalytical skills, tact, articulation and empathy.

A zillion examples of tight situations could be addressed in this chapter and we still might not jiggle your particular tightrope. Just be aware that it exists. And be prepared.

Case Study

One of the most difficult things to deal with is egocentrism on both sides of the tightrope, and there was an incident at the college that prefectly illustrates this high wire act. This is the true story:

An art professor had some of his own work exhibited at the college. A reporter from the *L.A. Times* came to review the show. Now, you have to understand that this is Los Angeles, with umpteen gazillion art exhibits, galleries, etc. I was thrilled that the *Times* featured our show in the local section, even though the writer was just a reporter and not an art critic. The coverage even included a photo of the exhibit.

It was a nice story, but had a final sentence that could be considered slightly critical of the paintings. Only slightly—and only if you interpreted it that way.

The professor was incensed. He called the reporter and screamed at him. He called the reporter's boss and demanded the writer be fired. The reporter called me. The reporter's boss called me.

I did my best to placate the writer, who was very upset. Unnerved, even. I explained that this particular professor was sensitive about his art work, that I was very happy with the coverage, and that I would tell the reporter's boss to ignore the whole thing. The reporter said it probably was the last time the *Times* would cover an exhibit at our college, and couldn't I keep "my people" under control? I didn't tell him it was also the first time his paper had visited an art show at our campus. Anyway, I finally soothed his feelings. His boss, incidently, was amused by the whole situation and we had a good chuckle over it.

Then it was time to confront the professor. I explained the reporter was not an art critic and was just trying to cover a local event, give the college some nice publicity and encourage people to come see the exhibit, and that he didn't mean to write anything that sounded critical. I said I thought the story and photo were very nice. I said in the future it would be better if he came to me when he had a complaint because media relations are very important to the college.

The professor pouted and grumbled, said he appreciated my efforts, but was still upset with the reporter.

Since then, the teacher has retired, the reporter has moved on, and the *Times* has never covered another art exhibit at the college. Sigh.

I hasten to add that the professor's attitude was an anomaly. For example, theatre arts faculty members teach their students that critical reviews are part of the process and should be accepted in the spirit in which they are written. Perhaps the art professor should have taken a drama class.

Related Web Sites →

www.biz.yahoo.com/prnews
www.7up.com
www.att.com
www.bankamerica.com

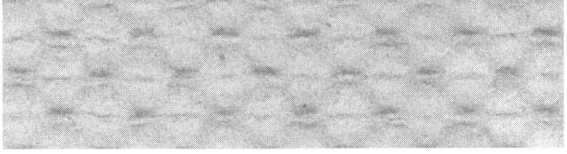

EXERCISES

Name_____ **Date**_____

1. "How come that reporter criticized MY department's swap meet on TV? He doesn't know what he's talking about! This is some of the best stuff I've ever seen. I'm going to call his producer and complain!" That's what you hear from the supervisor of your computer company's accounting department, which has worked hard to put on what amounts to a huge garage sale with some homemade crafts thrown into the mix. There are 500 employees, none of whom are actually working artisans—just hobbyists—including the accounting department supervisor. Most of the stuff is fairly mediocre, but the event is important to those who put it together. YOU were pleased any media covered the swap meet at all. Write a short essay explaining how you might defuse the situation.

Name_____ **Date**_____

2.   A new managing editor at your local daily comes to the job with preconceived notions about your large paint-manufacturing business. He's sure your employees sneak out at night and dump toxins into a nearby river. Actually, your company is very conscientious and has been "green" for a long time. Write a short essay detailing how you might convince him to change his mind.

3.   What major points should you make in a media communications seminar for your tobacco company's middle-level managers?

Section Two

General Practice

Chapter 8

Setting Policy

As we have mentioned in previous chapters, it's imperative to have in place a company public relations plan or policy. Some of the specifics of that policy, of course, will vary with the nature of your organization or the types of clients you represent. But there are many basic PR fundamentals that should be incorporated into the plan so you or your department can function effectively.

The PR Firm

If you work at a public relations firm, the media communication policy probably will be different from that of a regular company or organization. After all, we have to assume almost everyone working there is a PR specialist, right?

The PR firm's policy will be more concerned with procedures and rules appropriate for the company's clients. But a public relations business has to be concerned with its own reputation, too, so great care should be taken in formulating the regulations. And there will be those on the payroll who perform ancillary duties, who probably should be cautioned not to initiate media contact or answer reporters' questions.

Companies and Organizations

If you (or your department) are responsible for your company's or organization's public relations efforts, you must explain the advantages of effective media relations to the powers that be. (See Chapters 5 and 6 covering the development of credibility and training your bosses.) The CEO or governing body must be encouraged to recognize the wisdom of and implement the following basic ten-point PR policy.

> ### *Basic Company PR Policy*
> 1. The PR specialist will be privy to all agendas and related developments that may affect the organization's image.
> 2. All events or situations with the potential to affect the company's image will be reported to the PR specialist (or designee) immediately, even during non-office hours.
> 3. The PR specialist will be consulted for advice when any official decision or action is considered that may affect the company's image.
> 4. The PR specialist will be the organization's principal spokesperson when dealing with the media. Others within the company, after proper PR training, may be designated official spokespersons with specific areas of expertise.
> 5. All company spokespersons will be instructed by the PR specialist on effective media relations practices.
> 6. The PR office will initiate all official written and oral communication with the media and will be at least consulted for advice about written, graphic or broadcast communication with the public.
> 7. The company's disaster-preparedness plan will include a PR component for media relations during a natural or image-damaging catastrophe. All employees will have a copy of the plan and will understand their duties in that situation.
> 8. All employees are free, but not required, to speak with reporters on any matter, as long as non-designated employees do not represent themselves as official company spokespersons.
> 9. All employees will have a list of organization spokespersons—and their areas of expertise—to which reporters may be referred for official comment.
> 10. Reporters will be encouraged but not required to contact the PR office first.

Additional components in your company's PR policy should deal with specifics related to the organization's unique attributes.

Clients

If you are a PR consultant, you will operate with a different set of guidelines. And you will have a different set of problems—with clients instead of bosses and co-workers.

Whether your clients are politicians or actors, companies or cities, shopping malls or school districts, you constantly must deal with the potential for disastrous media relations.

The reason? You have less control over the actions and words of clients and their families and entourages than you do as an in-house PR specialist.

When a client hires you to handle PR, it is wise to sit down with that person and lay out some ground rules. Make it clear that the client, the client's spouse or significant other, the client's bodyguards, the client's employees, the client's campaign manager, the client's agent or attorney, etc., must follow the guidelines you advise or you will not be responsible for the results.

A contract agreement to that effect is an excellent idea.

It is imperative that you handle all media contact, unless your client has an abundance of natural PR abilities.

Your policy, which clients need to understand thoroughly, should encompass the following basic PR fundamentals:

Basic Client PR Policy

1. The PR consultant will be privy to all agendas, decisions, actions and related developments that may affect the client's image. If the consultant's advice is not taken and the results are less than satisfactory, the consultant has no responsibility for the situation.

2. All events or situations with the potential to affect the client's image will be reported to the PR consultant immediately, even during non-office hours.

3. The PR consultant will be the client's only spokesperson when dealing with the media.

4. The client will avoid media contact until he/she or the CEO has undergone training by the PR consultant.

5. Others within the client's "family" are encouraged to avoid media contact unless specifically trained by the PR consultant.

6. The PR consultant will initiate all official written and oral communication with the media and will be consulted for advice about direct mail and advertising communication with the public. If the consultant's advice is ignored, the PR specialist is not responsible for the resulting situation.

7. A client company/organization will have a disaster-preparedness plan that includes a PR component for media relations during a natural or image-damaging catastrophe. All staff or family members will have a copy of the plan and will understand their duties in that situation.

8. Client company/organization employees are free, but not required, to speak with reporters on any matter, as long as they do not represent themselves as official spokespersons.

9. Client company employees will be encouraged to refer reporters to the PR consultant/firm for official comment.

10. Reporters will be encouraged to contact the PR consultant instead of the client.

Additional components in your PR policy should address specific situations unique to your client list.

Case Study

After several attempts to devise an official media communications policy, I decided it would be better to have a small, user-friendly booklet called Media Relations Guidelines for Glendale College Employees that could be kept on every staff member's desk. It might be resented—and thus ineffective—if it wasn't subtle and tactful, so that's why I called it "Guidelines" instead of "Procedures" or "Policy" or "Rules."

I knew what information needed to be included in the pamphlet. That was the easy part. What was difficult was presenting it in gentle language that would persuade my co-workers to go along with the program. I also had to make it attractive, easy to use, and easy to read and understand.

It was organized into eight 8-1/2 x 5-1/2 pages. The topics (one to a page) included why the booklet existed (to help them deal with the media), some information about the media, psychology, what to say to reporters in different circumstances, what to do in an interview, who the designated spokespersons were, and some don'ts. It also emphasized our open-campus policy, where everyone is free to speak to reporters but not free to represent themselves as official spokespersons.

I ran it by my own staff, whose good judgment I trust, and re-wrote the thing at least ten times before I was satisfied. Then I chose a sort of lime green (hard to miss) cover and had the booklet printed on campus. The paper stock was standard bond, and just two sheets of 8-1/2 x 11, folded in half, made the eight pages. The green paper also was 20 pound bond. A couple of staples in the middle, and voila!, we had our guidelines.

After we distributed the booklets, I waited for feedback. Would there be a negative reaction? Nope. Nothing but positive comments.

Related Web Sites

www.xyber.se
www.commerce.com/nova
www.cyberpr.com

www

chapter eight

Name_____ **Date**_____

1. You have just been hired to handle the PR for a top-of-the-charts "gangsta rap" group. The DJ has a reputation for belligerent confrontations with reporters, another member of the group has an extensive prison record for armed robbery and other crimes, and a third is married to a very vocal mud wrestler. What specific terms would you add to the basic policy contract?

2. Your non-profit organization suffers from too many cooks in the kitchen, so to speak. Everyone has an opinion and gives it freely, especially to reporters. Some employees go to the press to complain about other staff members. This results in conflicting information going out to the public. What specifc terms do you add to the basic policy to resolve the situation?

Name_____ **Date**_____

3.   Despite your best efforts, your CEO remains clueless about media relations. How do you tactfully revise the basic policy to prevent her from continuing her destructive practices?

4.   Your client is a clown. Literally. You've both signed the basic contract, and you've done your best to encourage him to adhere to the policy; but he continues to stimulate negative public reactions by spouting off to the media. Do you terminate the relationship or try to revise the policy contract, and why?

Chapter 9

The Contact List Data Base

One of the most important things you must do as a PR professional is develop and maintain an updated contact list of all the media with which you deal. The scope depends upon the scope of your practice and could include anyone from local reporters to producers of national shows. Keep in touch regularly and update the information as soon as there are changes in staff, phone numbers, or whatever.

Your contact list should be kept on a computer disc (or a data base, if you prefer) for easy updating, and it must be printed out every time there's a change. Make sure there are hard copies to post in your office, keep with you, put in the emergency kit, etc. The names and fax numbers from the list also need to be in your fax-modem mailing program; and that, of course, also must be updated regularly.

News/Wire Services

News and feature services are the most expedient media for getting out a message fast to TV, radio and newspapers. There are international, national, regional and city "wires," and you must determine which ones are appropriate for your contact list.

You can get in touch with these services by fax, by phone to the "budget" hotline recording, by phone with a call to the budget desk, by mail or e-mail—so all of that information should be included on your contact list. (*See Fig. 9.1*) If there's a bureau in your area, that should be your initial contact rather than headquarters.

News Service	Budget PH	Desk PH	Fax PH	E-Mail
Associated Press-L.A.	555-9998	555-9988	555-9889	@ap.com
Address: 3333 Hollywood Blvd., Los Angeles, CA 90909				
Bureau Chief: MAX HEDRUM Assistant: LOIS LAYNE				
City News Service	555-7778	555-7788	555-7887	@CNN.com
Address: 2222 Main St., Los Angeles, CA 90908				
Bureau Chief: BETTI DAVID Assistant: SOUPY MANN				
Reuters - L.A.	555-8887	555-8877	555-8778	@RT.com
Address: 4444 Century Bl., Los Angeles, CA 90907				
Bureau Chief: MEL BOOK Assistant: BARTH SIMPS				

Figure 9.1
Sample news/wire services contact list

Weekly	Office PH	Fax	Address
Town Bulletin (Wednesdays; deadline 3 p.m. Tuesday)	555-7606	555-7609	333 Main St., Town, TX 90909

Position	Name	Home PH	Notes
Publisher	John Jones	555-7906	Conservative
Mng. Ed	Mary Smith	555-7066	Wants local only
Sports Ed	Bill White	555-5600	Needs photos & stats faxed
Gen.Rptr.	Bette Boop	555-6509	Slow, needs repeats
Gen.Rptr.	Stan Mann	555-6905	Wants feature ideas
Gen.Rptr.	Manny Mote	555-6699	Likes controversy

City Cryer	555-2233	555-2244	22 Broad Wy., City, TX 90910
(Wednesdays, Saturdays; deadlines 5 p.m. Tuesdays, Fridays)			

Position	Name	Home PH	Notes
Editor	Mary Jones	555-4422	Fair-minded
City Ed	John Smith	555-4321	Wants advisories only
Gen.Rptr.	Bill Boop	555-4230	Police Beat
Gen.Rptr.	Stan White	555-3412	School Beat, incl Sports
Gen.Rptr.	Bette Rite	555-2143	Council Beat, needs help

Figure 9.2

Sample local newspapers contact list

Local Newspapers

Weeklies

Local weeklies traditionally have small, underpaid and often inexperienced staffs, but that does not mean they are not read by the public. Therefore, it is in your best interest to cultivate a professional relationship with these people.

Your contact list for weeklies should include publishing days and deadlines, the names of all reporters, their "beats," their editors, the office phone number, the office fax number, the office address, and a home phone number or two. (*See Fig. 9.2*)

The list also should include the reporters' and editors' preferences, needs, and shortcomings. For instance, perhaps the city editor prefers advisories to news releases, or maybe there is no staff photographer, or possibly one of the reporters is hopelessly biased against ecological stories. Whatever the situation, these little notations should be kept on the contact list.

Dailies

Small dailies also tend to have underpaid, small staffs; but these papers also are read by area residents for local news. As with the weeklies, you need to cultivate the editors and reporters that may cover your company or client.

Again, your contact sheet should include all the pertinent information about deadlines, phone numbers, addresses, preferences, etc. (*See Fig. 9.3*) However, you may not need to know everyone on the staff—just the city editors and one or two reporters who cover your organization.

Daily	Office PH	Fax PH	E-Mail	Address
Nome News	555-6767	555-7766	@nn.com	333 Highway Rd., Nome, 80808

(morning; no Sundays; deadline 7 p.m. previous day)

Position	Name	Home PH	Notes
Mgn.Ed	John Boop	—	Likes opinion pieces
City Ed	Bette Jones	555-2345	Wants local calendars
Gen.Rptr	Mary White	555-5432	City Council Beat
Gen.Rptr.	Stan Rite	555-4352	Gen. Assignment

Figure 9.3
Sample local daily contact list

Metro Daily	Main Number		Address		
Miami Sentinal	800-555-2113		213 N. Beach, Miami, FL 70707		

Desk	Name	Phone	Fax	E-Mail	Ddln	Notes
Op/Ed	Joe Black	555-3322	555-3324	com@.jb	4 p.m.	Cranky
Arts	Ellen Elk	555-3345	555-3347	com@.ee	6 p.m.	Wnts clndrs
Police	Frank Fry	555-3312	555-3310	com@.ff	8 p.m.	Wnts quotes
City	John Rite	555-3300	555-3301	com@.jr	8 p.m.	Advisories

Figure 9.4
Sample metro dailies contact list

Metro Dailies

Large metropolitan daily newspapers focus more on regional, state, national or international news, so if your company or client needs that kind of coverage, you'll need to make contact with the appropriate "desks" at those publications.

Metro reporters tend to specialize, are well-paid (compared to smaller papers) and generally are more experienced and professional in their approach to news gathering. However, sometimes they also have bigger egos than their counterparts at the weeklies, so you need to be aware of personality quirks.

Your contact list for metro dailies should include the same general information about the papers; but deadlines, phone numbers and fax numbers probably will vary with the "desk." (*See Fig. 9.4*)

Television

Local News

Whether they're on an independent station or a network affiliate, most local news shows have the same types of stories, needs, preferences and deadlines. The focus will be regional and visual, and so should the story ideas you submit.

The list should include air time and length of broadcasts, plus any particular emphasis for each show. For instance, perhaps the noon show has more features. (*See Fig. 9.5*)

Station	News PH.	Fax No.	E-Mail	Address
WKAB Ch.8	555-9933	555-9936	@kab.com	29 Main St., Anytown, NY 10101

(News: 12-12:30 p.m., 4-5 p.m., 6-6:30 p.m., 11-11:30 p.m.)
Notes: Noon features, 4 p.m. interviews.
Day Assignment Editor: Nelly Norm, X9933
Eve Assignment Editor: Norman Jones, X9934
Weekend Assignment Editor: Betti Wright, X9932
Weather: Jack Frost, X9944
Arts: Mary Smythe, X9945

Figure 9.5
Sample TV—local news contact list

Show	Phone	Fax	Address
A.M. Philly	555-6565	555-6566	77 Sunset, Phila., PA 20202

Topics: City scene features, light.
Airs: Mon-Fri, 9-10 a.m., WRRR Channel 8 live in studio.

Producer	**Ext.**	**Assistant**	**Ext.**
John White	22	Mary Jones	23

Figure 9.6
Sample TV local talk/specialty shows contact list

Network	Producer	Phone	Fax	E-Mail
NBC Nightly News	John Smith	800-555-7788	800-555-8877	@nbc.com

Address: 1000 5th Ave., New York, NY 10101
Airs: 6:30-7p.m.   Notes: Doesn't like features.

Figure 9.7
Sample network news contact list

Local Talk/Specialty Shows

If there are any local TV talk shows or talk/entertainment programs, one of your clients might be a suitable guest as an expert on some topic or as a celebrity. Guest appearances usually are arranged by the show's producer or assistant, so you'll need to keep an appropriate list, with notes. Include cable programs. (*See Fig. 9.6*)

Network News

Network news producers are looking for topics that would be of interest to a large cross-section of the country. If there is a network-owned station in your area, then its assignment editor would be your contact. (*See Fig. 9.7*) If you're in a more remote region, you'll have to go for the network news show's producer. In the latter situation, you'll need to think ahead and give the producer enough lead-time to send a camera crew to your part of the country.

News Radio	News PH	Fax No.	E-Mail	Address
KFWW 97.0 AM	555-3377	555-3373	@kfw.com	560 Century, L.A. 90909
News Director: HUGH BEAR		Assistant: MIKE MARKY		

Figure 9.8
Sample radio all-news stations contact list

Talk Show	Phone	Fax	E-Mail	Address
Ice Q Show	555-4455	555-4454	@iq.com	40 Brand Bl., Brand, MI 30303
Airs: Mon-Fri 10-11 a.m.; WNNN 87.0 AM				
Topics: Current affairs, ethnic emphasis				
Audience: Middle class African-Americans				
Producer: SALLY JONES Assistant: BOB BARNEY				

Figure 9.9
Sample radio talk shows contact list

Network Talk/Specialty Shows

In some ways, it's easier to get a client on a network talk or specialty show than on the news. Producers always look for experts or someone to put a special spin on a national story or trend. In any case, you would contact the producer or assistant, and your contact list would look the same as the one for local talk shows. If you have time, you might want to send the producer a mug shot of your client, a copy of the client's book, or some other visual aid.

Radio

Local radio formats usually fall into one of four catagories: music, talk, sports or news. The predominant format is music, of course, and news on those stations normally is relegated to a couple of minutes every hour—if at all—and is taken from a news service wire. Unless your clients are involved in something related to music, or sports, you probably wouldn't have any contact with those stations. But all-news and talk-show formats could be useful for PR purposes.

Your contact list for all-news stations in your area should include the news director, assistant, phone, fax and address, plus any notes about preferences. (*See Fig. 9.8*)

For talk shows, your contact will be the producer or assistant producer, and you'll need to keep tabs on air times, topics, audience demographics, etc. (*See Fig. 9.9*)

Magazines/Trade Publications

As we noted in previous chapters, magazines come in all shapes, sizes and areas of interest. It's more difficult to get a mention in a national general-interest magazine than it is to achieve client coverage in a local or topic-specific publication. Depending on your situation, you'll want to develop contacts with the appropriate publishers or editors. It takes days, even weeks to put together a magazine, so deadlines will be an important part of your contact list. Audience demographics, circulation and favored subjects also should be included. (*See Fig. 9.10*)

Magazine	Main Phone	Fax	E-Mail	Circ
Rolling Spin	800-555-4466	800-555-4664	@rs.com	750,000

    Address: 2000 5th Ave., New York, NY 10101
    Publishes: Every other Friday
    Deadline: 2 weeks in advance
    Audience: Young adult males, middle class, 40% college grads
    Topics: Pop music, movies, politics
    Notes: Advisories only
    Publisher: KIP WUNDER X 4467
    Mng. Edtr: WANDA WEEKS X 4472
    Music Ed: NARDO BANKS (F) X 4475

Pipes	555-1133	555-3313	@pp.com	25,000

    Address: 100 Oak, Montgomery, AL 40404
    Publishes: Quarterly
    Deadline: one month in advance
    Audience: Pipe-fitters union members in So. U.S.
    Topics: Plumbing advances, promotions
    Notes: Will accept written stories.
    Editor: BOB PLUMB

Figure 9.10
Sample magazines/trade publications contact list

Radio PSAs	Phone	Address
KLLL 96.0 AM	555-4477	774 Hope St., Portland, OR 80808

    Public Service Director: SANDY HOPE
    Audience: General (pop music)
    Format: 20-, 30-second spot on 5-inch reel, 1 hard copy

TV PSAs	Phone	Address
WBOB Ch. 8	555-7743	347 Nile Ave., Boston, MA 60606

    Public Service Director: BOB NILES
    Format: Color slide, 20-second hard copy (2)

Figure 9.11
Sample PSA contact list

Public Service Announcements

Radio and TV stations will accept public service announcements if they're done properly; and sometimes, depending on the circumstances, PSAs can receive a lot of air time. Most radio and TV stations have a Public Service Director, and this will be your contact person. Audience demographics sometimes are a factor and should be mentioned in your list notes.

The contact list should include what physical types of PSAs the station will accept. For instance, perhaps only 20-second written spots will be used by a radio announcer. Or maybe the TV station wants a color slide and a 30-second pre-recorded voice-over. (*See Fig. 9.11*)

Case Study

The Glendale College PIO Media Contact List is divided into six sections: print, TV, radio, wire, ethnic, and VIP. Each list is kept in a separate computer file so that updates on one do not require printing out the entire thing.

Updates are frequent: new phone numbers, new fax numbers, new reporters or editors, new e-mail addresses, beeper numbers, and new news organizations (or at least new to our list), and new PIOs for fire, police, city, county, etc.

We keep the original files in Pagemaker, because that is our principal desktop system at this time. A data base program would be more efficient, perhaps, but also more difficult to output on easily readable pages.

It is essential that we have updated hard copies with us at all times, because we never know when or where we'll need the information.

The names and fax numbers also are kept in our fax-modem program, which at this printing is ProComm Plus. Thus, whenever we need to fax a media outlet, we simply call up the name and it's sent automatically.

Having the list in two separate programs requires double updating when there are changes, but it's the most efficient system we have at the moment.

I also have the original contact list and the fax list in my computer at home. Changes on the original list are modemed back-and-forth between my home computer and the main computer in our office, or hand-carried on diskette, so double updating is not necessary. However, I do have to update my home fax file independently.

Just a few years ago we didn't have this capability, but we've eagerly jumped on each new technology as soon as we could afford it. We learn as we go. Information is moving faster and faster, and we have to keep pace.

Related Web Sites →

www.latimes.com
www.abc.com
www.members.gnn.com/the
bighump/wabc.htm
www.kcbs2.com
www.bombsite.com
www.mtv.com

chapter nine

EXERCISES

Name_____ **Date**_____

1. Class project: Using the radio stations in your area phone book (all the call letters start with K or W), do a contact list for public service announcements.

2. Class project: Contact a local daily and put together a contact list of all the reporters and editors.

Name_____   **Date** _____

3. Class project: Contact a TV station news department and prepare a contact list of all relevant reporters and assignment editors.

4. Class project: If you have the appropriate hardware and software, enter the above information into a fax directory.

The News Release

The news release (*see fig. 10.1*) is perhaps the most well-known of all public relations products. But despite its advantages, the so-called publicity release actually has limited practical use.

When to Use It

Editors of weekly newspapers, small dailies and sometimes trade magazines will make use of well-written news releases. In fact, frequently these articles will appear with little or no editing—if a publication has a small staff and relies on PR professionals to fill in the holes with news briefs. Occasionally a really small paper will even run a feature story verbatim, especially if you provide a local angle and good photos.

Editors of small publications also will use your news releases as leads and assign reporters to develop them into more detailed articles.

However, sending news releases to larger publications, news services or the broadcast media is virtually pointless—unless the stories are provided as "background" and accompanied by a cover sheet media alert or advisory (see Chapter 11).

Professionals with large news organizations are bombarded by publicity releases—many of them bogus, poorly written or exhibiting little news judgment. Editors and reporters simply have no time to wade through all that paper, so most of those PR efforts automatically are relegated to the trash can.

Appearances

Before we jump into the specifics, some thought must be given to APPEARANCE. We're not suggesting style without substance, but an untidy, visually unappealing news release can interfere with the communication process.

Ergo, your news release letterhead should be clearly marked NEWS RELEASE and also should show the company or organization name and logo, the address in small type (perhaps at the bottom of the page), the company phone and fax numbers, your office title (Public Affairs, Public Information Office, President, Vice President of Marketing, etc.), and, if appropriate, your name and title and office phone number. That's a lot of information, so it needs to be arranged attractively.

Then, before the actual story begins, you should include some additional data on the page: name of writer, title of writer, release date, mail/fax date and some sort of headline.

Example

Mary Jones	Mail/Fax Date:
Editorial Assistant	Jan. 5, 2000

**RENO POLICE TO OFFER
ADULT CPR TRAINING**

Then begin your news release. Make sure it's double-spaced and try to avoid hyphenating words that don't quite fit on a line. There's no need to justify the copy because a ragged-right format is easy to read.

If you have the equipment, use a desktop publishing system. It looks better. If you must, at least type the release. Not even the smallest newspaper will accept hand-written copy.

If you need to go on to another page, center the word "MORE" or "OVER" (depending on your policy for saving paper) at the bottom of the first page. In the upper left-hand corner of the second page, use one or two words from the headline, add a couple of dashes, and then put "Add 1."

Example: RENO CPR—Add 1

At the bottom of the story, center several pound signs (#####) or put -30-.

How to Use It

News releases and feature stories normally are created to persuade the media to publicize upcoming events, cover an on-going situation, provide accolades for achievements or give the community information about a previous event.

Whether the release is sent to a small paper or trade magazine for publication, or accompanies a media alert/advisory to a large paper, news service or the broadcast media, it must exhibit good news judgment and be written in the most professional journalistic style.

We've discussed the importance of news judgment in a previous chapter. Now it's time to delve into the mechanics of good writing.

The Mechanics

Proper grammar, spelling and punctuation are essential. If you're not sure about something, take the time to look it up. And carefully proofread everything before you send it out. To do otherwise is to present yourself and your organization as less than professional, because grammatical errors and misspellings undermine your credibility. If this book was filled with such mistakes, wouldn't you begin to doubt the veracity of the author's words?

Style. In journalism, "style" does not refer to the reporter's trendy clothes. Style is the way in which certain things are presented in print: time, dates, money, etc. For example, three dollars is written, $3. The time is not expressed as three o'clock in the afternoon but rather as, 3 p.m. All of these rules are contained in the *Associated Press*

NEWS RELEASE

FROM THE PUBLIC RELATIONS OFFICE

123 Any St., Anytown, CA 23456 • 888/555-4567 • fax 888/555-1234 • email: msmith@cchow.com • web: www.cchow.com

Contact: Mary Smith
VP, Public Relations

Mail/FaxDate:
July 12, 2000

**CYBERCHOW TO THROW FREE
PICNIC FOR HURRICANE VICTIMS**

CyberChow employees will hold a free family picnic July 21 for victims of the June hurricane.

"So many people are displaced," said secretary June Budge,"and we wanted to do something to help them."

Festivities will run from Noon to 3 p.m. at CyberChow Park, located at the corner of Melrose and Vine.

All area families are eligible to attend, provided they present at the admission gate a snapshot of their damaged or destroyed home.

"We can't do much," said Budge, who spearheaded the effort, "but we can volunteer our time to cook food and run games and pony rides for the kids. The response from our staff has been marvelous."

Food, drinks and pony rentals have been financed by the CyberChow company.

"We've always been good neighbors," said CyberChow CEO Bart Bugle, "and this is a time when we all must put out a little extra effort to help one another."

#####

Figure 10.1
Sample news release

Style Book, which is the "bible" for most publications. Of course there are other style books, and many newspapers and magazines have their own peculiarities; but you'll be safely within most guidelines if you employ AP style in your releases.

Broadcasters, when writing scripts for TelePrompTers or voice-overs, use a totally different style designed to ease the process of reading aloud. To continue with our examples, "three dollars" would be written out and so would "three in the afternoon." But you should still use AP style when sending a backgrounder release to broadcasters, because that is the industry standard.

The News Release

A professional NEWS release is written in the inverted pyramid format. That means the most important information is at the beginning of the story and the least important at the end.

This style was developed by Civil War journalists when stories were sent back from the front by telegraph. If the wires were severed during transmission, then at least the most relevant data got through to the newspapers.

Even today, a suddenly downed phone line or malfunctioning satellite could prevent complete transmission from a field reporter. And, if a story is too lengthy for its plotted space on the page, it simply can be snipped from the bottom. Thus, the inverted pyramid style is a tradition to which you should adhere.

The lead, or beginning, should contain the major facts: who, what, why, where, when and how.

Arrange the lead in an interesting manner to attract the reader's attention. For example, which sentence captures your eye?

1. At 3 p.m. on March 17 the City Council met and voted to increase parking ticket fees from $25 to $50 beginning March 20.

2. Parking ticket fees will increase from $25 to $50 beginning Saturday as a result of Wednesday's City Council vote.

3. City Council members voted Wednesday to increase parking ticket fees from $25 to $50 beginning Saturday.

The first lead begins with irrelevant information. The second puts the most important fact first, but the sentence is awkwardly constructed. The third is a good compromise.

From there, fill in the rest of the information in decreasing order of importance. The story should be written in a precise and concise manner, with no extraneous words and phrases.

PR practitioners should be extremely careful not to include prejudicial adjectives, superlatives or judgmental words and phrases in news releases. If, for instance, you describe a company executive as "brilliant," your credibility goes down the drain. Instead, try putting that description in a quote from someone—preferably someone who at least seems impartial.

The Feature Story

Basically, there are two differences between a news release and a feature story. One is obvious: the letterhead should announce, FEATURE STORY. The other is the writing format.

Case Study

The Glendale College PIO sends out lots of news releases, especially to smaller newspapers, who make good use of the articles. Our releases always are written in a professional manner—devoid of superlatives—and we believe that is why they frequently are published without editing.

A good example is the annual campaign to publicize the Dance Performance. It should be noted here that the Dance Theatre is filled to capacity for each show, so there is no trouble getting an audience. But we view this event as a chance to enhance the college's image throughout Southern California, so we work hard promoting this truly excellent production. (OK, so I let a superlative creep in, but I don't do that in my news releases).

We begin early by taking many photographs of the dancers in various artistic poses. Twos, threes and groups. Our graphic artist, who's also the photographer, designs a poster using the best picture. She also designs a mailer, which is sent to everyone on the dance mailing list.

All the photos are then available to send out with news releases, and this is key when dealing with smaller newspapers.

I write a basic release with all the information and send it along with a photo or two to the local daily.

Another release with less information, plus a photo, goes to the two large metro dailies in Los Angeles. (Large publications don't have the space or inclination to print every name in the program.)

Those three papers also get calendar items, plus media alerts inviting reporters to attend a performance or take pictures during rehearsal. (Once a photographer showed up during a performance, but the head of our dance department didn't bat an eye. He simply showed the photographer the most advantageous place to stand that wouldn't be in the audience's way, and the next day we had a great color picture on the front page.)

But I digress. The fun part of this process is sending news releases and photos to all the dance students' hometown papers. (Every student involved in performance arts or sports is asked to fill out and sign a questionnaire giving us permission to use the student's name.) I utilize those questionnaires to group the dancers into various newspaper circulation areas, and then I compose different releases featuring those specific students in the story and headline.

It's a lot of work, but we get great coverage.

Related Web Sites

www.bulletin-intl.com/market/service.htm
www.caltech.edu/media/press_release.html
www.csmonitor.com
www.ndonline.com
www.columbia.edu/acis/bartleby/strunk

While a news release is written in the traditional inverted pyramid style, a feature story can be composed in a more relaxed manner. The rules of grammar, spelling, punctuation, AP style and page guidelines still must be observed, of course, but the most important facts do not necessarily have to go in the lead.

A feature lead is designed to grab the reader's interest.

"Do chickens really have elbows?" might be an imaginative beginning to a story about a poultry farm proposing to market chicken wings cut in two.

Use your imagination. Be creative (but factual). A well-written feature will be appreciated by the editor and the publication's readers. However, you still need to avoid extraneous words and phrases. Write tight.

Features usually contain more quotes and carefully selected adjectives (stay away from superlatives) and also could have punchlines or surprise endings. In other words, one important fact or notion could be held until the final line:

"Do chickens have lips?"

Internet

Also keep in mind the possibilities on the ever-expanding information superhighway. A vast and growing audience of local, regional, national and international bulletin boards is available—ready and waiting for your cleverly crafted message. But before you jump on your 'net surfboard, check out Chapter 18 for all the latest on cyberpublic relations.

EXERCISES

Name _____ **Date** _____

1. Write a news release using the following information.

Friday, May 12.	8 p.m. dancing.	7 p.m. dinner.	6 p.m. cocktails.
Buffet.	No-host bar.	Elks Lodge	

    Go Fish Country Band.   Sponsored by Ft. Worth Presidents' Club.

    $50 per person. $90 per couple.   No tickets at door.

    Fundraiser for Hospice Center for Terminally Ill Children.

    All-you-can-eat chicken (without elbows or lips).   Square dance.

    Reservations call 555-555-5555 or 555-555-7777.   Deadline May 8.

    Chairperson Mary Monk.   Caller Hoot Hoyt.   334 Main St.

    Goal to raise $50,000 this year.   Band donating its time.

Name_____   **Date**_____

2. Write a feature story using the same information as exercise no. 1.

Name_____ **Date**_____

3. Write a news release using the following information:

American Red Cross serving victims of earthquake   Vera Cruz, CA
18,000 temporarily homeless (homes damaged)   first 24-hour report
6,000 permanently homeless (homes destroyed)   4,000 housed in tents
3,833 injured   892 dead   5,368 meals served in 24 hours
regional director John James   tents set up at Smokey Bear Park
1,000 housed at Bear Park High School   10,000 gallons drinking water dispensed
blood needed   blankets needed   non-perishable food needed
contact local Red Cross to donate   hotline victim messages 888-555-1111

4. To whom would you send this release?

Name_____   **Date** _____

5.   Write a news release announcing the new CyberChow web site. (See Chapter 18 for sample home page.)

Media Alerts, Advisories, Calendars, Feature Ideas

In addition to the news release, other written methods of communicating with the press include media alerts, media advisories, calendar listings and feature ideas.

Each requires its OWN prominent letterhead to alert journalists immediately to the purpose of the communique. The other details on the letterhead should be the same as those on the news release.

Media Alerts

A media alert is a one-page brief outline of an upcoming event, advising the press of a story and/or photo opportunity.

If the event is within a day or two, a FAX MEDIA ALERT or e-mail should be used. The format would be the same, but the letterhead would reflect its FAX status and urgency. (*See Fig. 11.1*)

When to Use

Do not notify the press with a media alert unless the event warrants that kind of attention. Use your good news judgment. And, you'll need to consider WHICH media to alert. Is the event of widespread interest or just local? Is it visual for TV and still photographers? Should you notify specialty media or the ethnic press? Should the media alert be translated into other languages?

Don't forget about TV weathercasters and area morning shows. Frequently they like local footage of a colorful event as visual background, to broadcast from live, or to use as a feature.

The Format

As with a news release, your media alert should bear the name of the writer, the writer's title and the mail/fax/e-mail date.

Instead of a headline, you should specify whether this is a photo or story opportunity. And the information itself should be organized into a who, what, why, where, when and how format—easy to read. Background data can be listed briefly as the last entry, or you can note an attached news release if more information is needed.

Example

Contact: Kelly Smith	Mail/Fax Date:
Editorial Assistant	June 23, 1999

PHOTO OPPORTUNITY:

WHAT:	Groundbreaking for new Civic Center.
WHO:	Mayor Jan Groundhog, State Senator Bill Fox.
WHEN:	Thursday, JUNE 26 * 11 a.m.
WHERE:	Corner of Main and Holly Sts. (Press parking on west Holly)
VISUAL:	Hardhats, shovels, dirt.
DATA:	See attached news release.

Obviously, this example shows an event that would be of local interest only. The exact format will vary with the situation—note the "visual" and "data" entries and the mention of press parking.

Media Advisories

A media advisory differs from a media alert in that the advisory usually deals with a more sudden or serious situation.

Almost always this will go out as a FAX MEDIA ADVISORY or on e-mail. (*See Fig. 11.2*)

When to Use

A sudden development or announcement, an official statement on a serious matter, a physical disaster, or even a last-minute change in previous information given the press will warrant a media advisory.

In most cases, the first to be notified should be a news service because of the speed with which it can disperse your message. A fax or e-mail is better than verbal communication by phone because there is less chance for error or misunderstanding. Additional faxes should be sent to the appropriate media, if necessary. Keep this in mind: if an assignment editor sees your message on the wires and receives the same message by fax, that message will have added emphasis.

Format

A fax media advisory could take several forms. The letterhead should be as described above, and the writer's name, title and phone and fax numbers should be prominent, along with the date.

After that, it depends on the situation. If it's an announcement, it should be clearly labeled as such; and the person or company making the announcement should be named. Same thing for a statement, except it has to be made by a specific person. Be

FAX MEDIA ALERT

FROM THE PUBLIC RELATIONS OFFICE

123 Any St., Anytown, CA 23456 • 888/555-4567 • fax 888/555-1234 • email: msmith@cchow.com • web: www.cchow.com

Contact: Mary Smith
VP, Public Relations

Mail/FAX Date:
July 15,1998

WHAT:	FREE Family Picnic, including games & pony rides, for victims of June hurricane
WHEN:	Sunday, July 21 • Noon to 3 p.m.
WHERE:	CyberChow Park, corner of Melrose & Vine.
WHO:	Dignitaries: Anytown Mayor Bill Buck State Senator Jane Jones
WHY:	CyberChow employees want to do their part to help those whose homes were destroyed or damaged during the hurricane. Employees will cook all the food and run the games and pony rides.
HOW:	Admission requires a snapshoot of the damaged home.

Figure 11.1
Sample fax media alert

sure to mention the person's title. If it's a disaster, follow the guidelines in Chapter 27. Additional information may be faxed as an attachment.

Example:

Contact: Kelly Smith   Fax Date:
Vice President, Public Relations   July 25, 1998
PH: 555-6767
FAX: 555-6768

PLEASE ANNOUNCE ASAP:

The Hopscotch Galleria in Hazel City has closed for the day and will not reopen until 10 a.m. tomorrow morning, due to a police action that began at 2 p.m. More than 400 shops, including 5 major department stores, are housed in the Galleria.

Note to News Directors: For information about the police action, contact the Hazel City Police Dept.

Calendars

It should be obvious from the above example that calendars are much more pleasant to handle than media advisories. A calendar is a list of upcoming events or a single calendar item intended for a specific media listing. (*See Fig.11.3*)

When to Use

Many local newspapers publish calendars of events that are of interest to the community. Sometimes selected events are publicized on local TV or radio. If they get the information far enough in advance, magazines also publish calendars. And metro dailies frequently list events in categories such as "Stage, Opening Today . . ." You, as the PR specialist, must make every effort to get your organization's events included.

In addition, weekly or monthly calendar listings can keep reporters and editors advised about upcoming events they may want to cover. Either way, sending out calendars is usually a time-effective pursuit, especially if you use good news judgment.

Format

Again, the letterhead should announce, CALENDAR. The writer's name and title and the fax mailing date also should be prominently mentioned. The format itself may differ depending on the situation.

For instance, metro dailies are quite specific about the information they need for their calendars. The closer you adhere to their format guidelines, the better chance you have of getting your event in the listings. Observe deadlines. Direct the item to the correct "desk." It's worth the extra time.

General calendar listings always should include specific dates, times, places, any admission fees, and a few details of the event.

For example, this might be from the Blue River Police:

FAX MEDIA ADVISORY

FROM THE PUBLIC RELATIONS OFFICE

123 Any St., Anytown, CA 23456 • 888/555-4567 • fax 888/555-1234 • email: msmith@cchow.com • web: www.cchow.com

DATE: Jan. 1, 1998

TO: CARY CROSS, City Editor
OF: Midwest Clarion
FAX: 888/555-1255

FROM: Mary Smith, VP Public Relations

RE: CyberChow CEO's Statement about Errant Frog Leg

CyberChow CEO Bart Bugle announced today that a frog leg found in a Digital Dinner entree was placed there as a prank.

The employee responsible for the so-called practical joke has been fired.

"We take pride in the quality of our cuisine," said Bugle, "and I am horrified that anyone would do this. I apologize to our customers and I have already instituted new procedures to guarantee it will never happen again."

Bugle personally headed the investigation following the mysterious appearance of an amphibian's limb in CyberChow's newest Digital Dinner—Cajun Chicken & Carrot Stew. The leg was discovered yesterday by a woman who had prepared the meal in her DCD (digital cooking device). She called CyberChow, which immediately launched an investigation.

"The person responsible assured me only one dinner had been tampered with," said Bugle. "We are thankful for that."

Bugle said the name of the employee will not be released.

Figure 11.2
Sample fax media advisory

Example

Contact: Kelly Smith	Mail/Fax Date:
Community Service Officer	June 1, 1998

CALENDAR OF EVENTS
WEEK OF JUNE 23, 1998

June 23, Sun:	"CPR Training for Adults," presented by Chief Harry Green, 1-4 p.m., Room 2, $10.
June 25, Tue:	"CPR Training for Kids," presented by Chief Harry Green, 1-3 p.m., Room 2, $5. Ages 8+.
June 26, Wed:	"Say No to Drugs," film, free admission, 7-8 p.m., Room 3.
June 28, Fri:	"Police Ball," fundraiser, prizes for best costumes, 8-12 p.m., Elks Lodge, tickets $25.
June 29, Sat:	Community picnic, softball; 1-5 p.m., Elk Field, admission $5.

Internet

Don't neglect the growing information superhighway. If you have an event to publicize, announce it on the appropriate local/regional internet bulletin boards. For a thorough discussion of cyberPR, see Chapter 18.

Feature Ideas

Many beat reporters and their editors rely on ideas from credible PR professionals. "What's happening?" "Anything interesting going on?" "I need to fill a hole on the page!" These requests are not unusual on a slow news day, so you need to be prepared.

Better yet, stay ahead of them. Provide feature ideas on a regular basis (but not so often that it's annoying). Again, you need to keep track of who wants these "leads" and who doesn't. Don't forget the broadcast media and the ethnic press.

Format

The letterhead should say FEATURE IDEA(S) or FEATURE SUGGESTION(S). Include the contact's name and title and the mailing date.

Sometimes it's a good idea to use an attention-grabbing headline. Or, if you're listing several ideas, perhaps you could find a common thread and use that in the head. Try to match these leads with the specific newspaper or newscast. If you have to alter the words a little for each one, it's worth the effort.

See *fig. 11.4* for a feature idea that would be appropriate for both print and broadcast media. It's a feel-good human-interest story, uncomplicated, with lots of visual potential. If it was handled correctly, this one might even make it onto the network news.

CALENDAR ITEM

FROM THE PUBLIC RELATIONS OFFICE

123 Any St., Anytown, CA 23456 • 888/555-4567 • fax 888/555-1234 • email: msmith@cchow.com • web: www.cchow.com

Contact: Mary Smith   Mail/Fax Date:
VP, Public Relations   July 1, 1998

WHAT: FREE FAMILY PICNIC, plus games & pony rides, for
            victims of June hurricane. Admission requires a snapshot
            of your damaged or destroyed home.

WHEN: July 21 • Noon to 3 p.m.

WHERE: CyberChow Park, corner of Melrose & Vine.

Figure 11.3
Sample calendar item

FEATURE IDEA

FROM THE PUBLIC RELATIONS OFFICE

123 Any St., Anytown, CA 23456 • 888/555-4567 • fax 888/555-1234 • email: msmith@cchow.com • web: www.cchow.com

Contact: Mary Smith
VP, Public Relations

Mail/Fax Date:
Jan. 1, 1998

**CYBERCHOW FINANCE VP
COOKS UP TEDDY BEARS**

CyberChow VP of Finance Mike Marsh, himself the father of five grown children, says the worst thing about a fire is the soot- and tear-stained faces of little kids who have lost their homes. They need something to make them smile, and Marsh makes sure they get it . . . a teddy bear. A Marsh-Mallow Teddy Bear, to be precise. Marsh creates the creatures himself and adorns them with fire captain hats, and he makes sure the local fire stations have a good supply on their trucks at all times.

MIKE MARSH: Office phone: 888/555-7788
                   Home phone: 888/555-8899

Figure 11.4
Sample feature idea

Case Study

The White House contacted the Glendale College culinary arts department and requested edible Christmas ornaments for one of Hilary Rodham Clinton's trees. Other schools were asked as well.

We were very excited and wanted to alert the media, but the White House forbade us to do so until after Mrs. Clinton made the announcement and exhibited her all-edible decorations to the Washington press corps on a specific Monday morning at 10 A.M.

Even though that was 7 A.M. my time, I was prepared to confront my home computer.

The head of our culinary arts department had wisely directed her students to make many more ornaments than the number requested. Duplicates. And she had decorated a tree with them.

We arranged for her and some of her students to be with the tree beginning at 8 A.M. A photo opportunity. Interviews available.

My media alert was already written and ready to be faxed at 7 A.M. It said we were one of only a few culinary arts departments in So. California chosen to make edible ornaments for Mrs. Clinton's tree; and duplicates were adorning our own tree, which could be photographed beginning at 8 A.M. Plus the department head and students were available for interviews.

Of course, few reporters are on the job at that hour—print or broadcast. I waited awhile to begin my follow-up calls. "Did you get my fax about . . . ?"

Pretty soon we were in business. The local TV newscasts that night used network pool footage of Mrs. Clinton's tree and said Glendale College's culinary arts department made ALL the edible ornaments. (Ha!) The next day we had color photos on the front page of both major metro dailies.

What's that old saying about preparation plus opportunity equals success?

Related Web Sites

→

www.seatimes.com
www.pathfinder.com
www.holdcroft.com
www.fox.com
www.wtaetv.com

EXERCISES

Name_____ **Date** _____

1. Create a media alert for the following situation:

   Employees of Ned's Clothing Emporium have decided to have a fundraiser to help victims of a hurricane. This is Monday, April 2, and the event is Saturday (April 7) afternoon and evening. It will be held at Comet Park and will feature food (hot dogs and hamburgers, salads, watermelon, chips, sodas, ice cream, cotton candy), games (three-legged races, softball, dunk the mayor), pony rides, clowns, a palm reader, and, in the evening, the Country Joe Band, line dancing and hay rides. The event gets underway at noon and will end at midnight. Tickets at the gate are $5 for children 12 and younger, $10 for 18 and younger, and $15 for adults. You also have to think of a name for this event (perhaps something like The Round-the-Clock Country Jamboree?)

Name_____   **Date** _____

2. Write a media alert for the following event:

U.S. Senators Maria Sanchez and Jon Jung	Wednesday, April 4
tour of Bob's Orchards 1 p.m.	epitomizes plight of private farmer
picking apples on ladders photo op	3324 Orchard Road, Hadleyville
Both senators are Republicrats	pushing legislation for easing pesticide control
Bob Vasarian, owner, tour guide	not open to public

3. Write a calendar item for Exercise no. 1.

Name_____   **Date**_____

4. Write a media advisory for the following situation:

    | Bear Pacific railroad | derailment | 3 cars of 26 |
    | Pass and 125th Sts. | 7 a.m. | toxic fumes |
    | cause undetermined | source chemicals not determined | |
    | 2 injuries | Pass & 125th intersection closed until 2 p.m. | |

    To whom would you send this advisory, and why?

5. Get information about local performance (theatre, concert, dance) or art exhibit and write a calendar item.

Name_____   **Date**_____

6. Find a human interest story in your community and write a feature idea that should convince the local paper to investigate further.

7. You work for a PR firm. Write a media advisory about a news conference being called by your CEO to announce a new client. Use your imagination.

The Broadcast Media

Broadcast journalists are quite different from members of the print media because broadcasters, for the most part, operate under a different set of rules. Therefore, dealing with reporters from the electronic media can be a challenging experience.

But first, a few words from the sponsor . . . .

The FCC

TV and radio are regulated by the Federal Communications Commission, which awards and can withdraw licenses to broadcast over the publicly owned "airwaves." Ergo, TV and radio have to contend with FCC regulations, which ebb and flow with the political climate.

FCC regulations deal with such issues as obscenity, equal time for political opponents, and public service programming. In other words, broadcasters operate under restraints that are not placed on the print media. The First Amendment guarantees free speech and freedom from prior restraint for the press, but somehow the electronic media are not as protected as their print counterparts. This has been a bone of contention for some time. And with the advent of cable and satellite technologies, there are those who believe the FCC may have served its usefulness and should be abolished.

Ratings

In addition, broadcasters have been forced to compete for ratings. Both entertainment and news programming, and the growing number of shows that mix the two, are subjected to constant public opinion polls. A.C. Nielsen does it on the national level and Arbitron (radio only) regionally.

Nielsen and Arbitron weekly ratings ostensibly reflect what America is watching and listening to, based on a small sampling of the population. Techniques used include daily diaries and various metering devices. The ratings, especially during the quarterly "sweeps" periods, determine how much networks and stations can charge advertisers for air time.

Unfortunately, as we discussed in Chapter 4, the ratings to do NOT accurately reflect what Americans are watching and listening to; but because no better system has been invented, broadcasters and advertisers utilize the ratings anyway. Cable, satellite dishes, the remote control and the VCR, as well as the idiosyncrasies of the sampled public, all conspire to invalidate the findings. If and when interactive TV becomes widespread reality, the Nielsens probably will no longer be necessary.

News director Ronnie West in the KTTV control room

An engineer works in KTLA's master control room
Photos courtesy of the Daily News of Los Angeles

Other Differences

Newspapers and other publications place emphasis on the story and use photos or illustrations to make pages aesthetically pleasing, or charts to simplify a complex issue. The broadcast media, on the other hand, are principally interested in the visual aspect of a story and spend little time nailing down the details or investigating in depth.

As a PR professional, you need to know that a print reporter will be better prepared and will ask much more complex and probing questions. An electronic journalist will want something visual with a quick (20- or 30-second) sound bite. Under those circumstances, and with the added pressure of ratings, the broadcast reporter is inclined to go after a more sensational aspect of a story. And be forewarned: producers of those infotainment shows sometimes are not interested in facts at all.

Another difference between print and broadcast is the deadline. Newspaper reporters may have several hours to work on a story and magazine journalists may have days or even weeks. But the electronic media place great emphasis on immediacy, on broadcasting "live from the scene" whenever possible. Because of their deadline pressures, TV and radio reporters will put more pressure on you, will be more aggressive and more demanding. And, yes, sometimes more obnoxious.

The Key

The key to dealing with broadcast journalists (many of whom have no formal journalism training) is to remember what it is they want—and give it to them, on YOUR terms. Remember they are just people trying to do a job. Be cooperative and

KCAL anchor Leticia Ponce-Diaz hard at work during the evening news broadcast
Photo courtesy of the Daily News of Los Angeles

helpful. Be friendly and understanding. Be efficient. And be politely firm—don't let them push you around to the detriment of your client or organization.

Your attitude should be that you have nothing to hide (hopefully!), you'll help as much as is humanly possible, but you won't contribute to an inaccurate or slanted story. If you see things are heading in that direction, try to steer them away by making alternate suggestions.

Radio

In Chapter 4 we covered the media and how it works and in Chapters 10 and 11 we discussed communicating with print journalists. Now it's time to fill in the picture with additional information about the broadcast media.

Radio stations with music or sports formats, or even talk show formats, generally get their news from the wire services. It's the old "rip 'n' read" newscast, where the announcer rips the copy from the wire machine and reads it over the air maybe once an hour. Actually, few wire machines are still in use. It all comes up on a computer and you "scroll the wire." Ergo, if you want to get a message to their audiences, go through the news services.

All-news stations, however, have reporters who actually go out and cover stories. So if you have an event your news judgment tells you is appropriate for radio, then you must communicate that information directly to the station's news director—via the same type of media alert described in Chapter 11. Ditto for calendars of events and feature ideas. The media advisory could be more complicated: it's possible the news director will want an audio tape of any official statement, and that could mean taping you over the phone. Go with it.

KABC talk radio host Michael Jackson (L) chats with actor James Woods
Photo by Bill Lennert

Do not send news releases, unless they are attached as background for media alerts.

We discussed radio talk and entertainment shows and how to reach their producers in Chapter 9.

Television

Local TV news program personnel are sometimes difficult to deal with because their priorities can change on the spur of the moment. Of course this also is true with network news. Something bigger, splashier, more sensational or even more newsworthy might occur suddenly, and the camera crew you were counting on might be sent to another location.

Be patient. Complaining will be counterproductive in the long run. Just keep sending the assignment editor those newsworthy media alerts, calendars and feature ideas. As with radio, media advisories can be tricky. If it's simply information to be read over the air, that's no problem. But if it's an official statement on a hot topic, a media advisory could produce a camera crew in your office—demanding a sound bite. Use your best judgment. It could be the situation calls for a press conference. See Chapter 17 for details.

Again, do not send news releases to assignment editors unless they contain background material for a media alert.

Contacting producers for TV talk shows, both local and national, was covered in Chapter 9.

Ethnic Media

Do not neglect the foreign language electronic media. Areas with large concentrations of immigrants frequently have both radio and TV stations catering to their specialized audiences. If you have a message that needs to reach as many people as possible, you should contact foreign language stations as well as their English counterparts.

However, unless you or someone on your staff is multi-lingual, communication could become a problem. Usually foreign-language stations do have bilingual personnel to help translate, but you must be careful that the translation is correct. Otherwise, an inaccurate message could go out over the airwaves.

A perfect solution would be to send out media alerts, advisories, calendar items and feature ideas in the languages used at these stations. But if you don't have that luxury, try to make contact with someone at the studio who speaks English. Call him or her to make sure the communique is translated accurately.

Video News Releases

It's the age of information, computer chips, digital cameras, video cameras and visual emphasis. Thus, it's also the age of video news releases for the company with a big PR budget.

Betacams have become the industry standard, replacing the larger, heavier 3/4-inch portable cameras used just a few years ago. Although not yet in wide use, the digital camera is on the horizon. If you have super-VHS or 3/4-inch equipment, the editing bay to go with it and the facilities to dub your tapes onto the correct size—you can produce video news releases.

Using the same journalistic standards discussed earlier in this chapter, you can put together short (30 seconds to maybe one-and-a-half minutes) packages for your local TV stations. As is the case with print journalism, the smaller the news organization, the more willing it will be to accept and use your clips to fill out its broadcasts. But your package might also pique the interest of larger news operations and convince them to do their own story.

The possibilities are almost limitless.

Satellite Interviews

If you have the bucks and the proper equipment, you can arrange satellite interviews between your client and the broadcast media. Let's say your client has a new book and he or she is in New York. You can put that person in a studio, with an audio-visual hookup, and make him or her available for interviews across the country (or around the world) during a certain time span.

Case Study

The second largest broadcast media assault on Glendale College, at least in my memory, was provoked by a visit from a controversial California Supreme Court justice who was running for reelection.

When I found out Justice Cruz Reynoso was going to speak at the college, I alerted the media—by mail. This was during the Dark Ages before there were faxes. I followed up with phone calls to the wire services and TV assignment editors, to make sure they had gotten my media alerts. They had, but I couldn't judge from their tone whether or not they planned to send camera crews.

But on the morning of the big event, the white broadcast rigs descended on the campus like a pod of albino whales. Although I was basically a rookie PIO, I had already arranged for convenient parking—just in case.

As the justice walked from the administration building to the auditorium, he was set upon by microphone-wielding reporters and camera crews jostling for position. It was just like you see in the movies—ugly.

The Justice apparently was used to the media circus. He calmly answered a few questions and then excused himself so he wouldn't be late for his speaking engagement.

When he emerged from the auditorium a while later, the media swarmed up the steps. One of his aides asked me to intervene if the impromptu press conference got out of hand. I let him answer questions for about 10 minutes, then summoned my courage. As he finished a statement, I took his arm and said, "Thank you, Mr. Justice," and led him back toward the administration building. Amazingly, the reporters backed off.

I hope I appeared calmer than I felt. It was quite an experience.

Related Web Sites

→

www.searcher.com/links.html
www.tvnet.com
www.nielsenmedia.com
www.kfwb.com
www.kmgh.com
www.wcmh4.com

chapter twelve
EXERCISES

Name_____ **Date**_____

1. Using the same information given you for the No. 1 Chapter 11 exercise, devise a media alert specifically for television.

2. What is obscenity on the radio? Write a one- or two-sentence definition and then be prepared to defend it in class.

Name_____   **Date** _____

3. Write a short essay for or against the use of ratings for newscasts.

4. You work for a congressional candidate. Her opponent has received wide broadcast coverage recently because he rolled up his shirtsleeves to help deliver blankets and sandwiches to the homeless. How do you convince the news directors to give your candidate equal air time and emphasis?

Chapter 13

The Public Service Announcement

A cost-effective and relatively painless way to publicize a non-profit event or campaign is to make use of the broadcast media public service announcement. We stress: NON-PROFIT.

As we mentioned in Chapter 12, the FCC requires TV and radio stations to broadcast PSAs as a condition of keeping their licenses to use the public airwaves. However, because there are no rules about how often or when the PSAs should be aired, it could be once at 3 a.m. or it could be every day during drive time or prime time.

It's up to the person in charge, usually called the Public Service Director. Therefore it's up to YOU to make sure your PSAs follow the guidelines and appeal to the people making the decisions.

Radio

Some areas of the country have an organization that oversees the guidelines to be followed when submitting public service announcements. If that's the case in your region, the organization can provide you with details about what each station wants. If there is no umbrella group, you'll have to·contact each studio individually to find out about rules and regulations.

Keep in mind that some stations have brief community calendar segments each day instead of doing PSAs. In those cases, send a Calendar Item (see Chapter 11) to the proper person.

The Format

PSAs can be submitted in a written format (*see fig. 13.1*) or a taped format with written copy enclosed. A tape has to fit the specifications required by the station—5-inch reel, cassette, whatever.

Careful attention should be paid to the station's preferences. For instance, some stations might want only pre-recorded 20-second spots with one hard (written) copy accompanying each. Others might use only 10- and 30-second PSAs read by their own announcers, and they might need 3 copies of each. In addition, each station usually specifies lead time of from one to four weeks. In other words, if you want the PSA to begin on March 30, you might have to submit it on March 1.

If the PSA is REALLY important to your organization and you have developed a good relationship with the local Public Service Directors, don't hesitate to include a

KCAL news Spanish interpreters Miguel Rodriquez and Sari Bermudez work in the sound booth.
Photo courtesy of the Daily News of Los Angeles

cover letter stressing the message's importance to the COMMUNITY and urging that the PSA be aired often. But pick your spots—don't do this frequently.

The written copy should include the following information: name, address and phone number of the organization; name, phone number and title of the person submitting the PSA; start and stop dates; length in seconds of the PSA; the actual copy to be read; and sometimes a non-profit identification number or a number assigned by one of those umbrella groups.

Composition

As a general rule, a 30-second PSA has 75 words, it takes 20 seconds to read 50 words, and a 10-second PSA has just 25 words. It takes real skill to write an effective 10-second PSA!

The keys to an effective PSA, regardless of its length, are attention-grabbing words and repetition. Remember, your audience members can only listen, and probably while doing something else at the same time (driving, housework, homework, etc.). So you really have to get their attention, and you have to repeat key information as many times as possible.

You must eliminate all extraneous verbiage in order to leave time for the needed repetitions. Before you write the PSA, decide what the main message will be and stick to that. Then find a way to begin that immediately captures listeners' ears. Don't give complicated information—keep it simple. If a phone number is to be included, perhaps the digits can be expressed as a word that relates to your organization, like 555-HELP. And repeat that phone number several times.

Remember to make it easy for the announcer. Don't use abbreviations or symbols like dollar signs. Spell things out and phoneticize difficult words. Type it double-spaced.

An example of a 20-second PSA:

So what's your point? If you have trouble expressing your opinions, take advantage of HelpLine's free seminars next week. Learn to debate and argue successfully. Call 555-HELP today and register for one of HelpLine's free seminars. Make your point and make an impact. Call today. That's 555-HELP.

Television

Getting a public service announcement on television is more difficult than arranging a radio PSA. For one thing, TV air time is more valuable. A 30-second commercial could bring the station big bucks, but your 30-second PSA is free and brings the station nothing except, perhaps, good will (and fulfillment of FCC guidelines).

Therefore, it's your job to convince the TV station's Public Service Director to air your PSA as often as possible, preferably during prime time. That's not easy, but it can be done if you play on the person's community-mindedness or sympathies or whatever else that works. Be sure to emphasize this is an important message from a NON-PROFIT organization.

Another approach is to provide a high-quality tape that's ready to go. What could be easier for the Public Service Director? You've adhered to the physical requirements and made the video the exact length desired. All the engineer needs to do is put it into rotation and push the right buttons.

PUBLIC SERVICE ANNOUNCEMENT

FROM THE PUBLIC RELATIONS OFFICE

123 Any St., Anytown, CA 23456 • 888/555-4567 • fax 888/555-1234 • email: msmith@cchow.com • web: www.cchow.com

Contact: Mary Smith
VP, Public Relations
888/555-4567

START DATE: July 1, 1998

STOP DATE: July 20, 1998

READING TIME: 30 SECONDS

Did you lose your home during the June hurricane? We'd like to help! Bring the whole family to a FREE FAMILY PICNIC July 21 at CyberChow Park, on the corner of Melrose and Vine. Free picnic lunches, and free games and pony rides for the kids, too! Just bring a photo of your damaged home, and you'll all be admitted FREE! Come join us from noon to 3 o'clock on Sunday, July 21, at CyberChow Park.

PSA # 1111

Figure 13.1
Sample public service announcement

Case Study

One of our most successful PSA campaigns involved promoting the campus Citizenship Center. It's a unique program for anyone who has had a green card for at least five years and wants to become a U.S. citizen.

Our Center holds workshops to help people prepare for the naturalization exam, provides the photo and fingerprinting services, counseling, etc., plus actually administers the test right on campus. This saves immigrants the inconvenience of going to the Federal Building on L.A.'s west side.

When the head of the Center came to me for help in getting out the word, she was hoping for radio commercials. Well, our budget can't afford radio ads. But I suspected we could use PSAs to deliver our message, especially if we enlisted the help of Spanish radio stations.

I wrote the PSA and sent it to the Spanish language stations. Then I called and spoke to each public service director to emphasize how important this message could be to their listeners.

The PSA ran so often, other radio stations called and asked if I wanted to place a Glendale College ad during their drive time. They were amazed when I told them it was a PSA and not a paid ad.

As soon as the PSAs started to run, the Citizenship Center's three phone lines began to ring off the hook. Additional people had to be hired just to answer the inquiries. Every workshop was full.

The best successful campaign is a FREE successful campaign.

Related Web Sites

www.kbig104.com
www.radiokorea.com
www.rebelradio.com
www.werc960am.com
www.lava.net/radio-free
www.kron.com
www.wcovtv.com

Of course, you might not have the video and editing equipment necessary to produce a quality PSA. If that's the case, the alternative is a color slide mounted on glass and a written or pre-recorded voice-over. The slide will need graphics on it to emphasize major points like phone numbers, days and times, locations, etc. The station will then put the slide and voice-over on tape. But this is the old way of doing it, and you'll have more success with air time if you submit a pre-packaged tape.

Don't forget weathercasters and other local announcers frequently like to include some sort of PSA in their reports, so you could send them a video with graphics and a separate sheet giving the vital information. Don't put audio on the tape, and send it directly to the weathercaster or reporter.

Keep in mind that many local TV newscasts contain community calendars. Information for those listings should be submitted in written form and should be extremely simple: event, date, time, place and a phone number.

As for the content, TV PSAs usually are quite simple, but that doesn't mean you can't use your imagination. After all, it's a commercial, isn't it? Be creative. As with radio announcements, your TV message should grab your audience's attention and repeat the major points.

Don't forget the ethnic media—both radio and TV.

chapter thirteen

Name_____ **Date**_____

1. Write a 20-second radio PSA using the proper format and these facts: The non-profit Bob Foundation is holding an art auction Sept. 20 at the Museum Theatre. All proceeds go to college scholarships for art majors. Admission free. Reservations at 555-2787.

2. Write a 10-second PSA using the same information.

Name_____   **Date** _____

3. Read your local papers to find an upcoming non-profit event open to the public. Write a 30-second radio PSA for it.

Name _____   **Date** _____

4.   Write a plan for creating a TV PSA on the following event: Third annual Health Ride, sponsored by BikeAmerica, May 26, entrance fee $25 plus new stuffed toy, toys and funds for Children's Hospital, 9 a.m., 15-mile scenic route from Redwood to Pine, lunch provided, registration deadline May 25 at 888/555-2222, ride starts at Redwood's Bearcrest Park.

14

Direct Mail

Direct mail—communicating directly with the public—can be an effective public relations strategy that does not require the cooperation of the mass media.

It does require, however, an understanding of graphic communication, knowledge of and access to printing equipment, artistic skills, an understanding of mailing list usage and postal costs and a budget to put it all together.

Let's start at the beginning.

Saturation

You have a message you want to deliver to a certain audience. Your company or client doesn't want to rely on the media because you want to make sure the message gets to everyone in that audience. The most direct route is: direct mail.

Purpose

The first issue you should question is the purpose of the message. Is it strictly informational, or do you want the audience to act? Put another way: do you want to educate or persuade? Persuading takes more creative effort and probably a larger budget, so this is an important factor.

Budget

Another factor is budget limitations. Do you have an open checkbook or will you be required to keep spending down? Sometimes the size of the budget will determine the scope of your mailer.

A breakdown on the cost variables follows.

Direct Mail Cost Variables

1. DESIGN. If you have your own artists and typographers, the cost will be minimal for creating the camera-ready product. But if you have to go outside, even if you write the copy, you could have to pay for:

    A. Artist
    B. Typesetter
    C. Photographer
    D. Halftones or stats
    E. Graphic supplies

2. PRINTING. If you have an in-house printing department, your costs could be substantially less—if you can design a mailer your press is capable of printing. But whether you go outside or print in-house, the cost of supplies can vary widely. Some of the factors are:

    A. Quality of stock
    B. Size of stock
    C. Quantity of stock
    D. Number of ink colors
    E. Color separations
    F. Number of negatives and plates
    G. Trimming
    H. Binding

3. MAILING. If your company normally maintains its own mailing list, you can disregard that cost. But if you have to purchase a mailing list, that's more money. You'll have to decide if you want to send your message just to residences, or to businesses. Do you want to include apartments? How about post office boxes? Then someone has to put the labels on the mailer, organize everything into zip codes, bundle according to direct delivery to units (DDU) of local post offices and take the mailers to the post office(s). If you have an in-house department to handle all that, you're in good shape. If you don't, plan on giving lots of money to a mailing house.

4. POSTAGE. If you have 200 or more like pieces of mail that are organized properly, you can send them bulk-rate. The actual rate depends on whether your organization is officially non-profit or not, but it definitely will cost considerably less than the first class rate. The alternative is hand-delivering each piece to the public. There are companies that do that, and it is less expensive than postage; but sometimes hand-delivery is less reliable than the ol' postal service.

As you can see, direct mail isn't necessarily inexpensive. Still, usually it costs less than advertising in newspapers or magazines or on radio or TV. And the message goes directly to the audience you choose.

Message

Let's go back to our original question for a moment. Is the purpose of the message to inform or persuade? The answer will determine how creative you need to be and probably how much money you'll need to spend. Just remember—regardless of the purpose, your mailer MIGHT affect the audience's attitude toward your company or client. The quality

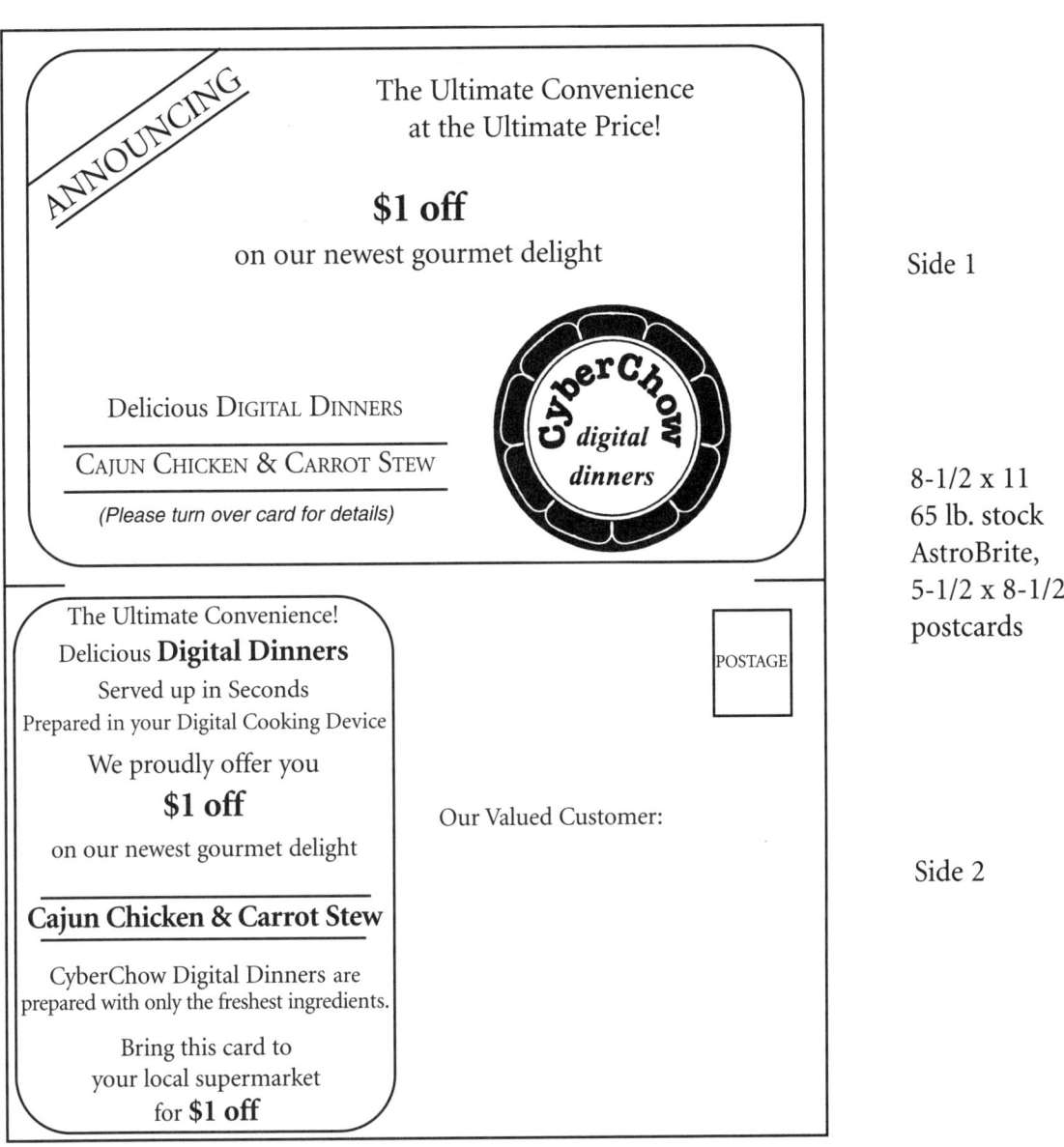

Figure 14.1
Sample direct mail

of the mailer and its message might cause some to feel more positive about your organization, or more negative, or simply reinforce an already-existing opinion.

The point is, even if your message is just meant to inform, you can't afford to publish a sloppy, unappealing, error-ridden mailer. That would reflect poorly on your client.

You also need to consider the way in which your audience will receive the message. Will it be buried in the junk mail or will it stand out as a separate piece? You should design the mailer with that in mind. If nothing else, it must be an attention-grabbing color and shape. Something must distinguish it from the rest of the mail. If it's not noticed, you can't deliver the message.

Then, you should make the copy and design appealing: easy to look at and easy to read. Eliminate excess words. Create an uncluttered look. Emphasize the key facts with attractive graphics. Direct mail can be very effective if it's done correctly. (*See Fig.14.1*)

Direct e-mail on the internet? We cover that in Chapter 18.

Case Study

Glendale College's biggest direct mail campaign is somewhat costly but far less expensive than the alternative.

We used to send the fall, spring and summer class schedules out to all the households in our area. Then two things happened: the schedules began to expand, and our budget began to shrink.

As more and more pages were added to the schedules, the price of printing them increased. At the same time, the State's budget for community colleges decreased; and all departments on campus were forced into some scary belt-tightening.

We decided to stop providing the class schedules free-of-charge. (At this time, they are $1 and about 100 pages). Now we can print far fewer booklets, and they pay for themselves through sales.

But we wanted to let the public know when the schedules were available and when enrollment would take place, etc. So I designed a 5-1/2 x 8-1/2 postcard to be sent out a few weeks before registration begins.

On one side is the same design that's being used on the cover of the actual class schedule. (Advertising art students compete for that honor). On the other side is registration information. We use gaudy stock to attract attention, and the postcards are printed on campus.

The cost of postage is less than it would be to send out class schedules, and postcards certainly cost less than printing an extra 100,000 schedule booklets. However, because it's the same number of pieces of mail, our bulk rate mailing service charges us about the same amount for that process.

Before we did the postcards, occasionally we would get complaints about "wasting taxpayer money" by sending out those bulky class schedules. Now we get complaints because we don't send them out and people have to pay for them. You just can't please everybody. (Welcome to public relations.)

However, once we reduced our direct mail expenditures, we never increased them again when the State began giving us more money. (The budget process is a real roller coaster.) Ergo, we really are saving taxpayer money, and we feel good about that.

Incidently, the PIO receives numerous requests from people all over the country who want our class schedules. Naturally, we don't ask them to drive in and pick up a copy, and it's too much trouble to ask them to send us a buck. So those people do get free copies mailed to them. But we think that's a small price to pay for good public relations.

Related Web Sites →

www.VirtualMex.com
www.infohaus.fu.com
www.imall2000.com

chapter fourteen

Name _____ **Date** _____

1. Contact a quick-print service and investigate printing costs for 20,000 two-sided 5-1/2 x 8-1/2 postcards in a 65-pound bright color, using one ink color and no halftones. Then ask for pricing for the following variables: typeset and design, one halftone, thinner stock, thicker stock, two colors of ink, and three colors of ink. Write your results here.

Name_____ **Date**_____

2. Develop an inexpensive mailer for a hospital that soon will begin offering free blood pressure screening. Indicate the following: size, shape, weight and color of stock; color of ink(s); mock-up of design with copy indicated in place. Remember, it's a mailer, so there has to be a place somewhere to put the label.

Chapter 15

Advertising

As your organization's public relations specialist, you may be called upon to create an advertising campaign or to coordinate your PR efforts with an advertising strategy.

In either case, you need to be aware of the options available and the cost variables.

We're not going to delve into the creative aspect of the advertising process. That's for another book. But you should know the services of artists, graphic artists, photographers, typographers, copywriters, camera operators, directors, editors and actors, as well as supplies and equipment, can be quite costly unless you have an inhouse department.

Print Media

Newspapers

Newspaper advertising can be effective if you want to reach the more educated members of the public. A general rule of thumb is to make your ad at least one-quarter of a page to attract attention. (*See Fig.15.1*)

Smaller local papers are read by community and opinion leaders. These publications are suitable for regional campaigns, and an ad on almost any page will do the job. Advertising rates usually are based on circulation, so the larger the paper the more you'll pay per column inch.

With metro dailies, pay attention to placement. Different sections traditionally draw different readers. Almost everyone scans the front page and catches a glimpse of the back page of the main section. Some will look at page three. After that, it depends on the reader's interests. There's the business section, sports, arts and entertainment, editorials and commentaries, international issues, local topics, popular culture or features, the comics, weather, perhaps a women's section. Select your ad's placement based on the audience you need to reach. Again, the larger the paper, the more you pay for advertising space. Just one ad could cost thousands of dollars.

Newspaper ads used to be, and occasionally still are, pasted up in the back shop.
Photo courtesy of the Daily News of Los Angeles

National newspapers, such as *USA Today*, are printed simultaneously in various parts of the country. Sometimes regional ad space is available, and sometimes you'll want to go for a complete run-through. This medium can be quite expensive, so it's best to use it for national campaigns only.

The Ultimate Convenience!
Delicious **Digital Dinners**

Served up in Seconds
Prepared in your Digital Cooking Device

Announcing our newest gourmet delight

Cajun Chicken & Carrot Stew

CYBERCHOW DIGITAL DINNERS
are prepared with only the purest, freshest ingredients

Try it today!
Available now in your local supermarket

Figure 15.1
Sample print ad

Magazines

As we've mentioned before, magazines vary tremendously in content and every other possible factor. And the demographics of magazine readers vary accordingly. So do the advertising rates. Depending on the publishing schedule, advertising deadlines can range from days to several weeks. You'll need to choose the most appropriate special-interest publication for your client or product. Because people spend more time reading magazines than newspapers, placement is not as important, although the back cover and inside front cover are coveted spots.

Trade Journals

Trades offer the most demographically pure audiences, and advertising rates generally are lower than those of regular magazines. City or chamber of commerce publications also are available at reduced prices and offer a specialized target readership.

And let us not forget the Yellow Pages! A display ad brings in more customers than a mere listing, so go for it.

Electronic Media

Radio

Radio advertising rates vary with the station's ratings and the time of day. Drive time is the most expensive because more people are listening. An advantage of radio advertising is that the station's format pretty much determines the demographics of the audience. Certain kinds of people listen to the news, others are hooked on talk shows, some prefer jazz to rap music, etc. Ergo, even though drive time ad rates are relatively expensive, radio can be a cost-effective way to reach target audiences.

Cable TV

Many local advertisers have discovered the simple, inexpensive world of cable. Cable operators take satellite-fed basic cable network programming and insert local ads during the commercial breaks. Please note: BASIC cable, not the premium channels.

You can run spots locally on, for instance, MTV, CNN and ESPN for a minimal price (generally $20 to $50 for 30 seconds). In areas where one cable operator has the franchise for the whole region, you can reach almost everyone. In areas where a number of cable operators divide the region, you'd need to run the ad on each one to reach everyone.

Some cable operators have facilities to help you produce a commercial for a relatively small fee. Otherwise, you're on your own. But if you want to advertise locally on a regular basis, it would be worth it to invest in a high-quality camera and perhaps even some editing equipment.

Just like special-interest publications, cable TV offers different target audiences. For instance, if you wanted to reach young people, you'd put your ad on MTV. ESPN is ideal for sports enthusiasts and has a high percentage of male viewers. Lifetime caters to women. CNN attracts opinion leaders. The audience should match your ad and your ad should match the audience.

Local TV

Advertising on local television can be expensive. Rates vary according to ratings, whether the station is independent or a network affiliate, and time of day. The most expensive time slots are during prime time, of course, and the least expensive are between midnight and 6 a.m. If you plan to advertise on local TV, you should plan to spend thousands of dollars. Use common sense. Buy time during programming that should attract the audience you're trying to reach.

Network TV

Network television advertising rates are outrageous, and only a national campaign is worth spending that kind of money. Again, prices vary according to ratings, time of day and whether it's a regular network or a basic cable network. Cable rates, as the technology spreads across the country, are catching up with regular network fees. As with local TV, buy time during programming that should attract the target audience you want to reach.

Movie Theatres

Talk about a captive audience! Advertising on the big screen is now available—usually in the form of 10-second color slides. Companies contract with theatre chains to provide this "service," so look for one of these companies in your area if you think movie ads are a proper outlet for your client. Prices are moderate.

Outdoor Advertising

Billboards, bus benches, busses themselves, some rapid transit, taxis and a plethora of other outdoor advertising possibilities exist. Rates vary with the exposure offered. With stationary spots, the audience comes to the advertising by driving, walking, jogging, skating or cycling in the vicinity. And public transit vehicles usually stay within a certain area, so in essence outdoor advertising offers little demographic stability other than regional location. That might be the ideal strategy for your client, however, so don't discard the possibility.

Direct Mail

We discussed the specifics of direct mail at length in Chapter 14, but more as a PR effort than as an advertising tool. Let us officialy note here, then, that direct mail can be used for advertising purposes as well. In fact, it's mostly used for advertising. All postal customers are inundated with catalogs, circulars and other pieces hawking products and services. You, too, can contribute to what many call junk mail. Just be sure yours stands out from the rest.

Cyberadvertising

Don't forget the web site as a cost-effective method of reaching a worldwide audience. It can be utilized as part of an advertising campaign or as THE advertising campaign — if you can get your web address in circulation, and if the demographics are appropriate. Check out the details in Chapter 18.

Case Study

The most cost-effective method of advertising for Glendale College is on cable TV. Not the public access channel, but on MTV, ESPN, CNN, etc. One cable operator owns the only system in the area, so that makes it simple for us.

Thirty-second spots are anywhere from $15 to $30, and that's really inexpensive—especially since we're getting our message to just the audience we want to reach.

Airtime is one expense for advertising on TV, and the other is production costs. But in our case, there are no production costs.

I create the commercials, with the help of our TV production professor. I use a Super-VHS camera, and we edit and do special effects in our own lab, where we also add Chyron (on-screen lettering), music and voice-overs. Then we dub the package onto 3/4-inch tape, which at the moment is OK for ads on cable. We're working on getting better equipment.

It's a fun process, especially since I compose the music at home on my synthesizer. And frequently friends tell me they "heard your voice on TV" because I do the voice-overs, too.

The content of the commercials varies, depending on which demographic we're trying to reach. For example, our campus research office determined that we needed to recruit more people just coming out of high school. So we ran a splashy, upbeat commercial on MTV and ESPN. The message was delivered in Chyron over stylized stills, with rock music. No voice-over. The message was that it was smart to come to Glendale College, where you could save thousands of dollars and get the same classes as those offered the first two years at universities.

We had nothing in place to measure how well the commercials were working. But we did have an increase in first-time freshmen.

As part of that campaign, we also ran ads in the local high school newspapers and yearbooks, which, for that particular demographic, is much more effective than placing ads in regular local papers.

Related Web Sites

www.bigyellow.com/home_yahoo.html
www.digimall.com
www.virtuallyeverything.com
www.Super.com.br/home/compras.htm
www.Austria.EU.net/sca

chapter fifteen

EXERCISES

Name_____ **Date**_____

1. Your client, a small shoe manufacturer, wants to test market a new aerobic shoe in your state. You are to handle the advertising, using as tiny a budget as possible. Which media would you choose to carry the message, and why? Then try creating a slogan and design that could be used in the campaign.

Name_____   **Date**_____

2. Lucky you! You get to create a national magazine ad for a new after-shave. And you get to choose the name. Describe and draw the ad here, including the copy and where it should go.

Name_____ **Date**_____

3. Write a 30-second radio ad for jeans. You create the brand name. Describe any sounds (music, background noise, etc.) other than voice and indicate if there is more than one voice. What kinds of radio stations have the demographics you need?

Name_____   **Date**_____

4.   Devise a 30-second commercial for MTV on your local cable. Let's say it's for a coffee house/espresso place. You create the name. Describe (or draw) what or who is to appear on the screen, write the script, and include what kind of music (or not) you would use. Have fun.

Chapter 16

Developing Experts, Getting Products Mentioned

Other methods for getting organization or client publicity include developing well-known experts within your company and getting your client or product mentioned in movies, newspaper columns and TV shows.

No doubt you've heard the old adage, "I don't care what you say about me, just spell my name right!" That may be true for those trying to earn recognition, but it's not necessarily true for those who've already arrived in the limelight.

In either case, your job as a public relations professional is to get your client or product mentioned in a positive way. And that can be a real challenge that tests all your communication skills.

Developing Experts

Every print and broadcast reporter probably will, at some time, consult and quote an "expert" or two to help explain a complex issue. Your assignment is to convince those journalists to consult YOUR experts, a situation which in turn will enhance the image of your client or company. The catch is you need to do the convincing ahead of time.

There are several ways to go about this:

Before you contact the media, make sure your experts truly are qualified, that they're willing, presentable and articulate, and that they've undergone your media communication training.

Then, send appropriate reporters and editors a list of your experts and their areas of expertise for future reference. Don't forget to include phone numbers, the best times to reach the subjects, brief bios and credentials and YOUR phone numbers. Make each "sketch" short and snappy and the areas of expertise very clear. Update the list frequently and send it to new reporters and editors.

Another way to attract attention to your client's "expert" status is to get him or her published in local or major newspapers and magazines. Encourage this person to write op/ed pieces, then edit them before they're submitted. Or you could ghost write the articles yourself if your client is more orally oriented. Then, when you send out your expert list, you can include copies of the published pieces. This seems to impress journalists, especially broadcasters, and could add credibility to your claims.

The KCAL news room is where writers research stories and create the TelePrompTer scripts.
Photo courtesy of the Daily News of Los Angeles

If a big local, regional, national or even international story breaks and you have an expert qualified to discuss the subject, immediately fax an "Expert Available" brief to all appropriate media outlets. Make sure your expert truly is available for the next few days. Although it's better to establish your experts ahead of time, it's possible some journalists will be desperate and on deadline and will consider your fax a gift from heaven.

Encouraging Client/Product Mentions

This strategy will require all your creative and persuasive skills. Have you ever watched a breakfast-table scene in a movie and wondered why the actors are eating and drinking brand-name products with their labels clearly in focus? How'd *they* do that?

Well, sometimes companies PAY to have their products shown. On game shows, for example, you might see "promotional fees paid by . . . " And other times the use of certain products just happens to be the whim of the director or producer or set decorator.

How does that happen? Perhaps the company's marketing department sent every director, producer and set decorator in Hollywood a case of the product. Or perhaps the company's PR specialist made it a point to meet, entertain and casually talk about the product with every director, producer and set decorator in Hollywood. As we said, this effort will require all your creative and persuasive skills, not to mention perserverance.

Getting your client or product's name mentioned positively in print or on the air requires even more effort. You'll need to convince columnists, editors, script writers and other whole categories of people. The trick is to get them to think of your client's name automatically *on their own*.

Case Study

When your community college is located in a megametropolis that supports some of the world's major universities, it's sort of difficult to get the media to notice your experts.

In our case, reporters have their choice of professors at UCLA, USC, Pepperdine, Occidental, and Cal Tech, to mention just a few. So the major media tend to gravitate toward them.

However, the local daily has discovered a gold mine in our faculty—accessible professors who are just as knowledgeable as their peers at the universities.

The most frequent requests are for those who are experts in some aspect of the social sciences and can comment on the issues of the day. Occasionally faculty members with opposing viewpoints and political perspectives are invited to debate on the local radio station.

One professor in particular is frequently in demand. He is an expert on Armenia and actually videotaped a running street battle there between opposing factions. He had to smuggle the tape out of the country, and he gets attention even from the major media. Another professor spends a lot of time south of the border and once hid in the hills with South American rebels while they were under fire. He calls me *compañera*.

Now the requests come on a regular basis; and I believe this new tradition is the result of a simple brochure I sent out a few years ago, touting our experts and their availability. Some sharp managing editor said, "Hey! We don't have to bother phoning UCLA and trying to track down some professor. We can call Merry over at Glendale College."

Well, maybe not. But I do try to send out those types of advisories every year or two, or when new reporters or editors are hired by the local press.

Related Web Sites

www.ucla.edu
www.usc.edu
www.pepperdine.edu
www.caltech.edu
www.movieweb.com/movie/top25.html

You must do a lot of preparation to make them believe it's their own idea. That could include casual but frequent mentions of the client's/product's good qualities, personal introductions to the client/product under favorable conditions, or perhaps just ingratiating yourself, as a representative of the client/product, with the people you're trying to influence.

The process almost qualifies as psychological warfare, and this type of public relations is not for the squeamish.

Sponsoring Charitable Events

Another method for achieving positive publicity is to sponsor or be one of the sponsors of a charitable event. Sometimes it's referred to as *strategic philanthropy*. This method costs money. Sometimes mega money. But your company or client name is exposed to not only the participants of, say, a golf tournament, but also to the general public through media coverage of the event. And it's positive exposure, because the proceeds are going to the local orphanage or to cancer research, or whatever.

Sometimes companies have to fight for media coverage, however, so you need to be aware of that. Here's an example: After Nissan began sponsoring the Los Angeles Open golf tournament, the event was called the Nissan Los Angeles Open. The media, apparently in an effort to appear uncorrupted by capitalists, kept calling it just the L.A. Open. Finally, Nissan got the name changed to the Nissan Open; and because that was the official title of the event, reporters had to include the car company's name.

It should be noted here that sometimes the media balk at using the full title of an event because the name is too long and cumbersome. Ergo, if you want your organization's logo included in the press, keep the event's title simple.

Just getting the name out there does not insure publicity about your charitable contributions, however. Many times reporters mention prize money (using the golf tournament as an example), but forget to tell about the rest of the funds that went to the Heart Association or homeless kids. So, when you're promoting an event, be sure the charity is high on the fact list.

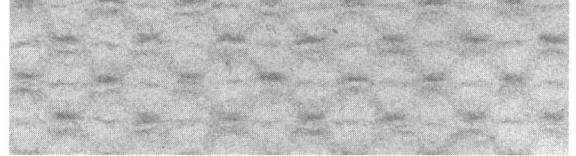

EXERCISES

Name_____ **Date** _____

1. Civil war breaks out between residents of northern and southern France. You have a client or company executive who is an expert on the history of internal conflicts in Europe. How do you get your expert on the air and mentioned by the print media?

2. Your client has a new car coming out, and you think a good way to promote it might be to have it featured in a prominent TV show. How would you proceed?

Name_____   **Date**_____

3. You've been hired by the Cape Flounder Chamber of Commerce to improve its image, and you've suggested sponsoring a charitable event. What kind of event would it be, what would you call it, and how would you promote it? Write your ideas here and be prepared to defend them in class.

The Press Conference, Press Kits and Speech Writing

Public relations professionals occasionally have to organize press conferences and develop press kits. Some PR jobs require regular media briefings, while others never involve that duty. But typically, the need for a press conference develops when you least expect it, so you should be prepared.

Press Conferences

When to Call One

When you call together the media to meet with you or your client, the occasion is called a press conference. It can be held at your place of business, a local press club, or any other location you choose.

Usually the purpose of a press conference is to make an important announcement and then allow the media to question you or your client. It's an efficient and effective way to handle newsworthy situations, for both you and reporters.

We stress: NEWSWORTHY. Do not call press conferences unless the situation warrants it, or your credibility, and the credibility of your organization or client, will be damaged. It's sort of like crying "Wolf" too often: when a truly important occasion arises, editors will ignore your summons.

How to Call One

If you've done your homework and your contact list is current and you have a good relationship with the media, calling a press conference should be no problem. Depending on time constraints, fax or phone every (and only those) news organizations you think would be interested in the topic. If time is really short, fax the wire service(s). In your fax, be sure to mention date, time, place, parking, the topic(s) and the name(s) and title(s) of the speaker(s).

When choosing the location of the conference, make sure there is ample room, lighting, electrical outlets, seating, water and phones.

There's nothing quite like the sight of numerous TV crews crammed together on a riser, with all their cameras lined up on sticks (tripods). Here they await a press conference by President Clinton.
Photo by Merry Shelburne

Still photographers, at least the legitimate news variety, are usually low-key and casual at a press conference.
Photo by Merry Shelburne

The meeting should be held at a time convenient for the media attending. Early morning usually isn't good, but 11 a.m. to 2 p.m. normally is convenient for deadlines— allowing time for writing and editing. Or, if you want the conference to be telecast live, hold it during a newscast hour.

How to Organize

You can prepare for the eventuality of a press conference by making sure possible speakers understand what to do, what to say, what to wear, etc. In other words, keep them updated on media communication guidelines.

Once the press conference has been called, it's up to you (and your staff, if you have one) to accomplish the following:

1. Brief speaker(s) on the topic(s). If there's anything potentially controversial or even unclear, try to get your stories straight. If there's a statement to be made, write it and make copies to be distributed among the media. You also should, if there's time, brainstorm about possible questions and how they should be answered.

2. At the press conference site, take care of the following:

   A. Arrange and mark the media area so there are designated spots and ample room for camera crews, photographers and reporters.

   B. Enough chairs for the press.

   C. Good lighting.

D. Microphones are in place and there is proper equipment and space for the broadcast media's own microphones. Electronic equipment is working: do a sound check.

E. If possible, and if it's warranted, auxiliary microphones are available in the audience area so reporters can hear other reporter's questions.

F. A podium, dais or table is in place for the speaker(s). If there's more than one speaker, be sure there are enough chairs.

G. The background behind the podium or table looks attractive and is appropriate.

H. Any visual aids, such as charts, overheads, slides, film strips, videos, etc., are in place, along with the necessary equipment.

I. Glasses of water for speakers and the media. If it's going to be a long session, you might provide coffee, punch or sodas, snacks, etc.

J. A bank of phones, with room to work by each one, in the conference area or directly outside.

K. A supply of handouts: statement(s), bio(s) on speaker(s), mug shot(s) of speaker(s), written material on your company, organization or client. (Note: See Press Kit below).

L. Other possibilities: Do you need an interpreter? Will the media want access to copiers, fax machines, typewriters or computers? Will there be anyone else the press might like to question?

3. Make sure your speaker is dressed appropriately. All black, all white, vertical stripes are to be avoided. Neat and professional is the order of the day.

4. When the media arrive, direct camera crews, photographers and reporters to their designated areas. Assist in setting up their microphones.

5. If there is any kind of delay, keep the press updated on the situation. And feed and water them.

6. When your speaker arrives, go to the microphone(s), officially open the conference by greeting the press and explaining any format or ground rules, and then introduce the first speaker.

7. After the presentation, the media usually will want to ask questions. Depending on the level of understanding and/or controversy, you might want to assist the speaker at this point. It might be helpful, since you know the reporters, if you control the question and answer period by calling on them one at a time as they raise their hands. Or, your speaker might be familiar with the press and would want to handle it.

8. When the question and answer period is complete, go to the microphone and thank the reporters for coming. The best policy is to stick around until all the journalists have asked every question they want. But there are times when, for instance, your client has another appointment and must leave, or perhaps the session has gotten out of control in some way. In those cases, you must step to the microphone, thank the reporters for coming and then escort your speaker out of the room.

9. Fax copies of statement(s) to the media who did not attend. Or, if time allows, send them a press kit.

10. If possible, it's a good idea to discuss the successes and failures of the press conference with your client or company executives. Then you can avoid making the same mistakes in the future.

Cyberconferences

The technology now exists for cyberpress-conferences on the internet. Check out Chapter 18.

Press Kits

We've all heard about press kits. They run the gamut from bags filled with gifts to folders with a simple news release inside. Sometimes press kits are handed out to journalists covering events, not just press conferences.

But whatever the situation, here's the plain truth: generally, REPORTERS HATE PRESS KITS! Especially the thick variety filled with everything even marginally related to the subject at hand.

Why? Because reporters are on deadline, and they don't want to wade through all that STUFF to get the information they need. They'd much rather ask someone and get a direct answer. They are not impressed with four-color foldouts and fancy brochures. And most are prevented by their news organizations from accepting ANY gifts, so those brandy bottles with your company logo will have to stay behind.

The Proper Press Kit

There are times when a lean, efficient press kit can be helpful to print journalists and, occasionally, to broadcasters. A simple folder will do. Inside could be a copy of an official statement or speech, perhaps a fact sheet in outline form, and maybe a photo of the person or product in question. That should do it, unless you want to include a sharpened pencil. Anything else is superfluous and annoying.

Of course, there are certain areas of media coverage that could require a more extensive press kit. Entertainment reporters, for instance, might like a brief synopsis of the film you're announcing. Sports writers could use a media guide filled with stats, facts and figures on the upcoming World Cup. Business editors would need your company's annual report. Political reporters might like the complete wording of the legislation you're proposing. But aside from these specific needs for specific journalists, keep your press kits simple.

Speech Writing

It may be your job to write the speech your client or boss delivers at the press conference — or anywhere else. If this is one of your duties, several factors must be taken into consideration during the preparation stage.

Although not all of these elements will apply all of the time, the following general guidelines will help you with the basics:

1. AUDIENCE. Identify the individuals or groups who will witness—either first-hand or second-hand—the presentation. What tone and style will appeal to them? Formal or informal? What kinds of words, phrases and symbols will communicate to them the message you want to deliver? What topics are of interest to them?

2. MESSAGE. Decide—preferably with input from the speaker—what message you want to impart to this audience. Is the purpose to entertain, to inform, or both? Outline several clear points you want to emphasize, and don't deviate far from the central idea. (Of course, you must take into consideration the length of time allotted for the speech. Given the brief attention span of many audiences, usually a shorter presentation is preferable.) Once you've identified the salient points of the message, put them in the order they should be delivered. Frequently it's helpful to have a summation at both the beginning and the end.

3. SPEAKER'S ASSETS & LIMITATIONS. A successful speech is written in the presenter's normal speech pattern or cadence. Remember this is an oral delivery: the audience cannot see the words. Also keep in mind any idiosyncrasies the speaker might have and try to capitalize on appealing traits while disguising the shortcomings. For example, if your boss or client tends to speak in a monotone, by all means write short, snappy sentences.

4. MEDIA. If print or TV reporters will be present, you'll need to incorporate good quotes and/or sound bites into the speech and have printed copies of the text available. If a question and answer period is to follow the presentation, you should attempt to anticipate what questions will be asked and rehearse the answers with the speaker.

5. INTERFERENCE. Try to gauge where applause might interrupt the presentation and indicate those spots within the text (but not on the copies distributed to the media). If you suspect hecklers might try to disrupt the event, be sure to warn your speaker.

6. APPEARANCE. The speaker's physical image could make or break a presentation. Your boss or client should be well groomed and must wear apparel appropriate for the situation, the audience and the message.

7. FACILITIES. Prepare any visual aids needed for the speech and be sure they are in place and operational. Do a sound check if you can. And, if possible, adjust lighting, background and dais position to suit your purposes.

Case Study

I'm happy to say we've never had to call a press conference per se, but I've occasionally had to rein in an overly enthusiastic administrator or faculty member who wanted to summon the media for non-newsworthy purposes.

We did participate in a joint press conference with the city. It was called to announce some sort of college-city effort to do something. I've forgotten what. In any case, the participants far outnumbered the reporters, who took up only three chairs. I knew that's what would happen, but I didn't want to be uncooperative. It only took a few days out of my life, anyway. Now the city has its own PIO—and a good one—thank goodness.

The college does summon the media for actual events, such as groundbreaking or dedication ceremonies. We have had a string of new buildings (paid for by the State), with more to come.

On those occasions, a simple press kit is necessary. I include a sheet with information about the building, when it will be completed, its cost, the names of the architect and builder, what the facility will house, etc. I might also include a small architect's rendering. Or, if it's a dedication, maybe a photo of the structure. And if I'm feeling really generous, the reporters will get sharpened Glendale College pencils and my business card. That's it.

Related Web Sites

www.prsa.org
www.adcouncil.org
www.ama.org
ftp://ftp.netcom.com/pub/sp/spj.html

WWW

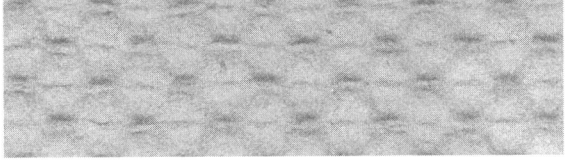

chapter seventeen

EXERCISES

Name_____ **Date**_____

1. Your client is a state senator who is running for reelection. He has proposed a bill that will help farmers in a small portion of the state, but the legislation is stalled in committee and isn't getting any attention from the media. Do you call a press conference? If so, when and where, and whom do you invite? Who will be your speaker(s)? How do you prepare them? Write a short essay.

2. Will there be a press kit? If so, describe what will be in it.

Name_____ **Date**_____

3. You've invited the media to dedication ceremonies for your company's new beer production plant. Do you have a press kit, and, if so, what should be in it?

4. Your CEO has practiced, he's performed his speech perfectly at the press conference, and he has handled all the questions as you rehearsed. But a reporter keeps trying to ask the one question your CEO doesn't want to discuss. How do you handle the situation?

Name_____   **Date**_____

5. Write a speech for the police chief who wants to convince the city council to provide additional funds for a new jail facility. The address, just five minutes long, will be delivered at a luncheon meeting of the local club, to which all the city council members belong. Your chief has no unusual speaking problems.

Chapter 18

cyber.pr

We've touched on the subject where appropriate, but now it's time for a thorough discussion of computer technology as it applies to public relations.
Go to http://www.coursewise.com/shelburne/

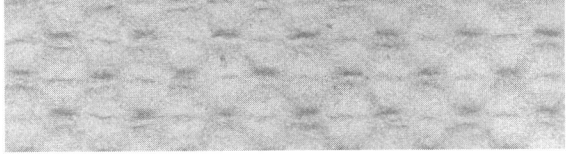

chapter eighteen

EXERCISES

Name_____ **Date** _____

1. Design, on paper, the home page of a web site for a city of 100,000. Invent the city name, a rough logo, and then draw a draft of the page. Write in the copy and note type style, colors, etc. Then explain why you have used those components.

Name_____ **Date**_____

2. Write a direct e-mail marketing message for a company that's building a virtual mall. Pay particular attention to the sender's name and the subject, because those two items need to entice the person to read the message. Invent the company's name. In a separate paragraph, explain to whom you would send the message and how you would obtain their e-mail addresses.

Name_____ **Date**_____

3. Design a fax cover sheet, including a rough logo, for the public relations office of the company of your choice. It can be a real company or one you invent.

4. If you have access to the internet, design your own personal home page. If you do not have access, design it on paper.

5. Plan, on paper, a complete web site. Include all the buttons and what other pages they would link to, and what would be on each page. Follow the guidelines for exercise no. 1. Make it a public relations type of site—no hard sales. The site should be for a retail company of your choosing, real or not.

Chapter 19

Dealing with Dignitaries

Occasionally you might encounter government types wanting to use your venue for political gain. They could be local, state or federal.

Your job as a public relations professional is to make sure your company, organization or client also benefits as much as possible from the dignitary's proximity. Or, you might want to invite officials to your site to call attention to a particular project or situation.

Either way, the bigger the office the person holds, or the more controversial the figure is, the more media he/she will attract. And media means exposure for your business.

Even White House officials may choose to visit your site. You never know where they might show up, especially during an election year. We'll discuss that later in this chapter, but first let's tackle the more likely scenarios.

Local Folks

Local officeholders offer the most frequent opportunity for *quid pro quo* activities. Mayors, police chiefs, city council members and school board officials usually are elected, and they benefit from favorable publicity.

If you forge a friendly alliance with these people, they'll visit your venue during auspicious occasions and bring the cameras with them. They'll also be in a position to perhaps throw some city business your way (all above-board, of course), or actually work with you on some projects. If yours is a non-profit organization, state or federal grants could be pushed in your direction. And all of these things could lead to stories and photo opportunities with the media.

Of course, only the local media will be interested, unless you devise some spectacular activity or human interest application. And if you work in a major metropolitan area, even the local press won't take the bait unless the story is truly newsworthy.

All of the above co-benefit activity is predicated on mutual good reputations. If the local official is in hot water, forget the joint project. You don't want your CEO in a photo with someone accused of misappropriating city funds. Nor will the mayor want to be associated with a company suspected of polluting the water supply.

State Officials

Unless you work in the state capitol, opportunities for mutually-beneficial photo ops will be few. For example, forget inviting the governor to an open house at your new child care center. However, if it's an election year and child care is a hot item on the incumbent's agenda, then the state's chief executive might show up—with the media in tow.

Ditto for state legislators. Perhaps your company is on the cutting edge of an industry some official wants to push. Or maybe he/she wants to attract federal grants to the state, and your client is particularly qualified to work on a special project. Those kinds of opportunities are perfect for media exposure.

In any case, it's a good idea to forge relationships with state officials so you know where their interests lie. Work with them where appropriate. For example, they support your project and you support their legislation, etc. (This effort might entail some trips to the capitol by you or your company's executives—for the purpose of offering your expertise on a particular subject, and, of course, a little *schmoozing*).

If you have good relationships with state dignitaries, they might actually accept your invitation to visit. Depending on the subject and what else is happening that day, you could get some positive exposure. But be advised that legislators frequently send aides from their local offices to attend functions for which their presence has been requested. Don't be too offended. The celebrity-less situation might adversely affect your carefully planned media coverage, but there's always next time.

The Feds

Visits from unelected federal officials probably will be infrequent, if at all. It depends on the type of organization you represent. But if your venue is chosen, at least for a positive reason, it's time to call in all of your media markers. This has the potential for major exposure.

Chances are your company has achieved something notable, or it exemplifies a program the government wants to emphasize, or you have been awarded some sort of contract or grant. (Or you have been very, very bad, in which case you should revisit your code of ethics.)

It'll be your job to simplify what might be a complex explanation for the visit, and get that information to the press before the event. Usually these things are not open to the public, so a Media Advisory or Alert would be appropriate. And remember— if the event is visually colorful, you could get some TV coverage.

If the national visitor is planning a press conference, remember that preparation is the key, and review the words of wisdom in Chapter 17. Otherwise just invite reporters to tag along.

Most congresspersons should be considered the same as state legislators in their potential to draw the media. They, also, can be cultivated by forging a working relationship. U.S. senators, however, are bigger fish and could provide quite a bit of press exposure, especially if the topic is a hot one. Again, make it your business to find out what issues concern them.

The White House

Chances are it won't happen to you, but you never know . . . .

One of the most challenging experiences a public relations practitioner can have is working with the White House press office—and the Secret Service—when your venue is the site of an executive visit.

Despite all the technological advances—cell phones, pagers, faxes and electronic mail—communication remains the biggest potential stumbling block in planning and executing a successful event.

The bottom line is that YOU must take as much responsibility as possible. YOU must be completely organized, because the White House press office isn't necessarily familiar with your local media. And YOU must be politely aggressive.

A helicopter delivers President Clinton, over the heads of the waiting crowd at Glendale Community College.

President Clinton delivers a speech at Glendale Community College after being introduced by Associated Students President Hazel Ramos.
Photos by Merry Shelburne

Still photographers, reporters and the public await President Clinton's address.
Photo by Merry Shelburne

Exposure

An appearance at your venue by the President, the First Spouse, the Vice President or VP's spouse, presidential candidate or a prominent Cabinet member can be a thrilling experience for the locals. It also offers the possibility of extensive positive exposure for your institution, company or client. If the White House calls, say YES!

Most visits of this nature, depending on the prominence of your guest, generate massive media coverage. You simply can't buy that kind of publicity, so you must do your part to make sure the coverage is positive. It's also an ideal situation for you to improve your own media relations.

Advance

It all begins with the White House advance team, which includes a lead press person, a Secret Service site administrator, and a person in charge of physical arrangements. Plus all of their staff members. There may be several weeks to prepare for the big event or only a few days, but the advance team will be around for all of that time. Count on experiencing the proverbial whirlwind of activity *plus*.

The first thing you have to understand is that the Secret Service has the final say on everything that even remotely affects the visitor's safety. *Everything*. That includes people. That includes YOU. Be prepared for background checks and interference in nearly everything you'd like to accomplish.

Once you've accepted that circumstance, get to work with the lead White House advance press person. In addition to handling the national press traveling with the executive, he or she will be concerned with three things: where to position both the local and traveling press at the venue, how to credential the local media, and where to set up the on-site White House press office the day of the event. Your input could be invaluable. Give it freely.

Media Positioning

The advance press person will make sure the traveling media have an excellent location for the speech or whatever activity is planned. Those members of the press already have security clearances and the Secret Service will be tolerant.

Your concern should be the positioning of the local media. Those are *your* reporters and camera people. You have to live with them after the pominent visitor is long gone. Do your absolute best for them, and let them *know* you're working hard on their behalf. Make sure they have as much access as the Secret Service will allow.

Pay attention to the amount of space available for camera crews. They might be put on risers and there should be enough levels to accommodate everyone comfortably. And make doubly sure there is a good line of sight. If camera crews will be allowed to move, find out ahead of time what the restrictions will be so you can keep them informed.

The same goes for still photographers. If they're compelled to stay in one place, lobby for an unimpeded line of sight high above the crowd, which probably will stand from time to time. Nothing is more irritating than trying to take pictures through people's heads.

Print and broadcast reporters should have comfortable seating with a good view. Again, it's imperative to find out ahead of time if local journalists will be restricted in their movements so you can keep them informed. Generally, they'll cooperate if they know the rules.

Don't forget to arrange for refreshments and a way to get those goodies to the media. The White House advance press person will take care of the traveling media's food and probably will set up an on-site filing center near the press office for those reporters. There may or may not be an on-site filing center for local journalists, depending on the time of day. But if it is determined there should be a facility for the local media, make sure there are phone lines, tables and chairs, goodies, etc.

Credentials

The nightmare begins. If you work in a large city, the number of media wanting to cover your event could be considerable. Even in a smaller area, every newspaper, TV and radio station within 100 miles could want to attend. In addition, there might be some surprises—journalists from national and regional news organizations that are not among the pre-credentialed traveling press. Then there's the network pool camera crew, which will be given the best head-on view of the scheduled activity. In short, every media person not part of the traveling press will need to be credentialed for your event.

If you have the staff to handle it, volunteer to take over the credentialing process. This gives you control and you're in a position to do favors for your local media. Always look at the big picture, remember?

So, where to begin? The White House advance person should have a stack of credentials pre-printed with the date of the event. These should be turned over to you, and your staff should keep them in a safe place.

The next step is to prepare a simple fax media advisory announcing the visit and giving details about getting credentials. Also include information about the nature of the visit (topic of speech, activity), whether or not the person will be available to answer questions, why your particular venue was chosen, etc. In addition, indicate the deadline for faxing a credential request to your office. Send it to everyone on your contact list, including the wire services and regional offices of CNN, etc.

Credentialing instructions should contain the following information: On the news organization's letterhead, each editor or assignment editor must give the name, date of birth, and social security number of every person being sent to the event.

Requests for credentials should start coming in right away, and you will have to keep a list, in alphabetical order by news organization, of all the media personnel. Include date of birth and social security number data. Periodically, turn over the updated list to the White House advance person. Keep the faxes for later use.

Some problems could occur at this point. For whatever reason, some news organizations will fax their credential requests to the White House press office in Washington, D.C., and others to the White House advance person's local office. Be aware of this and make arrangements to get those requests as soon as possible. No doubt you will be working evenings and weekends, so it would be helpful to have a computer and faxmodem equipment at home.

Next, prepare a fax media advisory to send out to the news organizations that have requested credentials. This fax should contain information about picking up those credentials. If possible, make the date and site the day before the event at your office. This gives you continued control and the opportunity to meet and greet your local press. In addition, include a map showing where to park, where to obtain the credentials, and where to park and enter the day of the event. Each news organization usually is allowed to send one representative to pick up all the credentials. That individual must have a photo ID issued by the news organization.

For the broadcast media, be sure to indicate where they can park their rigs, and also if and when *preset* has been scheduled. Preset works like this: broadcast crews are allowed to come to the site early and run cabling, set up their cameras on sticks (tripods), and arrange audio equipment. Then they have to leave the secured part of the venue for two hours while the Secret Service searches everything and brings in the bomb-sniffing dogs.

Another problem could surface at this point. Due to garbled communications between the White House press office in Washington, D.C., and the advance office, some news organization editors could receive inaccurate information from sources other than your office. They might claim, for instance, that they've been told they can pick up their credentials the day of the event. It's best to try to avoid these snafus by keeping in close contact with the advance person and Washington. Make sure all your stories agree.

Press Packets

Now you know who intends to come to your party, and you have the tickets. Is there a way to score additional media relations points? Yes! First of all, put each person's credential in a separate envelope, with the person's name on the outside. Then put all the envelopes for each news organization in a larger envelope. This makes the whole pick-up process easier.

In the individual envelopes, include your business card, a news release with the latest information, another map, and some sort of nice but inexpensive item that carries the name and/or logo of your organization, company or client. A sharpened pencil is nice. Or a pen. If your staff has time, print the person's name and affiliation on the credential.

Some larger news organization editors will have faxed you information about an entire list of people because they're not sure exactly who will be covering the event. In that case, find out *how many* credentials they need in their packet, but don't fill in any names.

Staff Credentials

Current White House policy is to allow the host company one still photographer and one video. The videographer will be put with the other camera crews and will have to be credentialed accordingly. The still photographer will be allowed to accompany the

White House photographer. This person will have to go through a background security check and will be issued a special pin to wear.

If you can present a convincing argument, you might be able to talk the advance person into allowing you additional photography and video privileges. This might be a once-in-a-lifetime chance to record a prestigious event for future publicity purposes. In any case, if your staff wears media credentials, they will be forced by the Secret Service to stay in areas relegated to the press. *Make arrangements for you and your staff to get security clearances and pins to wear,* so you can move around the venue without problems.

In addition, be sure to wear a badge of some sort that shows your name and identifies you as the venue's public relations officer. This will help with both the media and the Secret Service.

The Big Day (or Night)

Regardless of your best efforts, some media personnel will insist on picking up their credentials at the last minute. This means the day of the event you will have to set up a press check-in table with an appropriate sign. Someone from your staff should remain at the table until just before the activities begin. Most of the pencil press (White House name for the print media) will arrive a half-hour to an hour early. Broadcasters will be there even earlier to set up their equipment. Everyone will have to go through metal detectors each time they enter the secured area.

Try to make the media comfortable. Offer refreshments, etc. Even though you're not in control of the event, the party is at *your* house, and this is an excellent opportunity for *schmoozing.* Sorry, but it's true. If funds are available and there's enough time, a nice gesture might be giving all the media small gifts commemorating their visit. Perhaps a baseball cap with the company logo.

Be prepared for the possibility that the on-site White House press office will be of no help to you. That staff is principally involved in catering to the needs of the traveling national press. Your responsibility will be taking care of the locals. If a speech has been given, be sure to get copies of it for the regional media. Requests for additional information about such things as crowd size, etc., should go though you.

During the appearance of your guest, you might be asked to help police the press. That means cajoling them into staying where they've been assigned, commiserating with them about the restrictions, and most definitely answering questions about your company or client. Try to have a good time.

Afterwards

Remember those faxed credential requests you were instructed to keep? Imagine the gold mine of information they contain. New news organizations you didn't know existed. New assignment editor names. New fax numbers. Incorporate all of it into your ever-expanding contact list.

The White House advance press person probably will call you later for an assessment. Don't be shy.

If the service is available in your area, make arrangements to collect all the TV and radio news clips on the big event. And, of course, you'll want all the print clips as well. Put all of it together for the archives and for future publicity purposes.

Keep in mind it's also a record of your outstanding public relations achievement.

Case Study

You may have guessed it by now. Yes, President Clinton did deliver a speech at Glendale College—in June of 1996.

Seriously, I wish I'd had this chapter to read ahead of time!

Only my gut instincts, based on years of PR experience, pulled me through.

We had just five days to prepare. I knew it was an incredible opportunity for the college to gain national positive exposure. I also knew it was a great chance for the PIO to expand and enhance media relations. And I suspected the local (L.A.) media might get short-changed. So, I volunteered to handle credentialing.

The White House advance press guy was great, and we kept in fairly close touch. He gave me instructions about the procedures, and the blank press passes, and then left credentialling totally in my hands.

My staff and I worked our butts off. I worked all weekend, too, both at the college and at home. In the end, we had credentialled 150 journalists. There were snafus. There were people calling the day before the event insisting on credentials. There were journalists arriving before the specified time to pick up credentials, catching us with unfinished packets. There were constant phone calls about the President's speech topic and the reason he chose Glendale College (we didn't know the answer to either question). There were conflicting releases and conversations with the White House Washington press office.

I lost it. Several times.

I also made several mistakes. I should have paid more attention to the "overflow media site" for the pencil press and still photographers. It was at the top of an uneven hill, and when the audience stood up, the media's view was blocked. I also should have insisted on distinctive badges for myself and my staff. The advance guy left that in the hands of his assistant and staff, and they were, to be kind, less than competent.

We were instructed to arrive at 6 a.m. on the big day. The advance guy was with the President and traveling press in Santa Monica. The press office staff gave us nothing to do; and because we had no identifying badges, the Secret Service was less than cordial. So we twiddled our thumbs for a few hours.

It was a beautiful day. The crowd was in place, the flags were flying, and the music was playing. And then, like a scene from *Blue Thunder*, a United States of America helicopter suddenly rose above the administration building. The crowd of 2,000 (mostly faculty and students) went crazy. It was exhilarating.

The rest is a blur, except for the encounter I had with a Secret Service agent when I tried to step over a security line. And the complaints of the photographers when the audience stood up. My graphic artist/photographer got to hang out with the White House photographer, but the rest of us on the PIO staff got nowhere near the President.

Still, it was a banner day for the college, and we made some new friends in the media. We have newspaper clippings from everywhere and a videotape of all the mentions on the newscasts. CNN ran the entire speech live, and Glendale College was still being mentioned several days later. We also have a gazillion pictures that can be used for years.

It was worth all the effort, and it was a real learning experience for us.

Next time, though, I'll be better prepared.

Related Web Sites

www.Yahoo.com/Government/Politics/Humor
www.eit.com/web/www.servers/government.html
www.ncsl.org
www.whitehouse.gov/WH/welcome.html
www.foundations.org

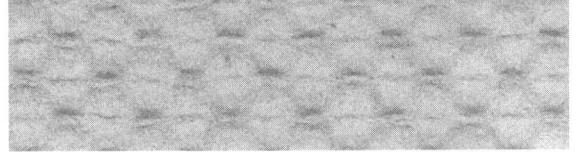

chapter nineteen

EXERCISES

Name_____ **Date**_____

1. You work for the largest vegetable-packing company in your small, rural state. The new packaging facility is, you hope, a prototype for all such buildings. It is faster, cleaner and safer for employees, and the quality control is unparalleled. Your company wants recognition during the dedication ceremonies. What dignitaries do you invite, and how do you promote the event? Identify and write each component of the plan.

Name_____   **Date** _____

2. Create a fax media advisory announcing a Presidential visit to your city's new microchip processing facility. Include the appropriate press credentialing instructions. Then write the second advisory about picking up credentials. Finally, indicate a plan for an individual press packet with the appropriate materials inside.

Name_____ **Date**_____

3. Write an invitation to your U.S. Senator, asking that she visit your company's new in-house child care facility. Be convincing.

Chapter 20

The Don'ts

You've been given lots of DOs and DON'Ts, so in the interest of clarity it might be helpful to have all the DON'Ts together in one place.

Here they are, in no particular order:

DON'T treat reporters as if they're obligated to give you publicity and ignore image-damaging stories.

DON'T tell journalists how to do their jobs.

DON'T complain to editors or broadcasters about mistakes, unfair emphasis, placement or headlines unless it's REALLY, REALLY important.

DON'T lie to the media.

DON'T call a press conference unless it's warranted.

DON'T plan news conferences early in the morning or late at night.

DON'T pester reporters or editors when your stories aren't run.

DON'T inundate the press with non-newsworthy releases and media alerts.

DON'T send news releases to the electronic media, news services or metro dailies, unless they're background for a media alert.

A definite don't: This is what happens when you don't give still photographers line-of-sight accommodations. *Photo by Merry Shelburne*

DON'T use "off the record" unless there are special circumstances and the reporter has agreed to it ahead of time.

DON'T say anything to a journalist that you wouldn't feel comfortable seeing in print or hearing on the air.

DON'T put anything critical in writing about specific members of the media.

DON'T let your company executives or clients interact with the press until they understand your media communication guidelines.

DON'T have anything to do with the tabloids.

DON'T pack your press kits with superfluous materials or gifts.

DON'T try to prevent your organization's employees from talking to reporters, but make sure they understand they can't represent themselves as official spokespersons.

DON'T make grammatical, factual, spelling or punctuation errors in written communication with the press.

DON'T make statements about a subject until you understand it.

DON'T ignore or delay returning reporters' phone calls.

DON'T waffle.

DON'T yell at, accost or throw objects at reporters. (Just kidding. You would NEVER do that, right?)

Case Study

I have a superb example of a "don't," but I'd like to keep my day job.

Related Web Sites

→

www.berkeley.edu
www.sandiego.com
www.u-tokyo.ac.jp

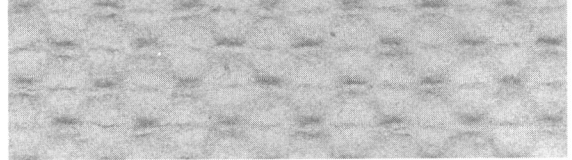

chapter twenty

Name_____ **Date**_____

1. Make a list of other DON'Ts that come to mind.

Section Three

The PR Campaign

Chapter 21

The Campaign: Set Realistic Goals

Before you begin a public relations campaign, first you must differentiate between what you WANT to achieve and what you realistically CAN achieve.

Should you try to get everyone to vote for your candidate, or would it be smarter to go after the "undecided" crowd and the independents?

Can you get every consumer in the nation to buy your client's product, or would it be more realistic to aim for a positive attitude adjustment toward the product's value?

Will you improve your organization's image by attempting to reach every citizen, or can you do it by convincing just community and opinion leaders?

As a PR professional, reality probably will be easier for you to recognize than it will be for your client or company executives to do so. Therefore, it's your job to convince them to set achievable goals.

Newspaper graphics and artwork are created on computer
Photo courtesy of the Daily News of Los Angeles

Setting Parameters

In addition to being realistic, your goal(s) must be specific, measurable and have a time frame. If your aims are vague, how will you know if you've achieved them?

Suppose your executives say they want the company to have a more positive public image in the area of environmental commitment? What do they mean by "more positive?" "Public image?" "Environmental commitment?" You'll have to insist on specific definitions, or the campaign won't get off the ground.

Do they mean a poll of community leaders (the public) taken now and an identical poll taken in six months (the time frame) would reveal a measurable difference in their perception (image) of the company's expenditures (measurable commitment) for environmental protection?

Now, that's a specific, measurable goal set within a time frame. You can work with that. You can plan a realistic PR campaign to achieve that goal.

Case Study

One of the biggest PR campaigns the college has done was actually more of a public information campaign.

For 65 years, GCC's fall and spring semesters began and ended at the same time as the Glendale Unified School District terms. In fact, until 1981, the college was part of the GUSD. Many students transferring from the college to a university complained that there was an overlap, so in the early 90s we decided to put our semesters in the same time frame as those at the California State Universities. We would start a month early, in August, and the fall semester would be over before Christmas vacation. The spring semester would run from January through May.

Our goal in this campaign was to make sure the public knew we were instituting an "early start," so that we would not experience a drop in enrollment. We needed to get this message to EVERYONE in our area. It was a realistic, specific, measurable goal within a time frame. (Continued at the end of the next chapter. . . .)

Related Web Sites

www.claritin.com
www.cocacola.com
www.pepsi.com

WWW

But sometimes things can get complicated. Suppose your executives have more than one goal in mind? And suppose those goals might interfere with one another? Suppose they want community leaders to believe the company is more ecologically responsible, but they don't want similar companies across the nation to know about it? Or, worse yet, suppose they want you to convince community leaders that the company is committed to environmental protection, but actually they don't plan to be environmentally responsible at all?

This is when you have to start talking fast and using all your logic and communication skills to convince them of their unrealistic assumptions. They haven't been paying attention to your communication guidelines. Perhaps it's time for another seminar?

You can handle more than one goal in a PR campaign, as long as they are not contradictory. But trying to devise a plan to deceive anyone is a really, really BAD idea. It WILL backfire.

The Plan

OK, so you've set non-contradictory, realistic, specific, measurable goals within a time frame. The next step is to define your audience. Read on.

chapter twenty-one

EXERCISES

Name_____ **Date** _____

1. For the purposes of this exercise, and those following in the next five chapters, create an imaginary non-profit organization. Think of a public relations goal for that organization and make sure it matches the parameters we discussed.

2. Do the same for a retail company.

3. Ditto for a politician or rock star.

Chapter 22

The Campaign: Define Your Audience

Once you've determined your goals, the next step is to define the audience you need to reach—the people you want to influence.

A public relations goal cannot be achieved in a vacuum. The process always involves an attempt to change the attitudes and, ultimately, the actions of people. Therefore, to reach a PR goal, you must successfully alter human perceptions.

But which humans' perceptions? To achieve your goal, do you need to influence the attitudes of every citizen in the country? Usually not. You need to reach the RIGHT people, not all the people.

So, you must decide which group of people can help you reach your goal. Whose altered perceptions will result in the actions you want taken?

Demographics

For example, suppose the Red Cross has a shortage of blood in county A, and the organization is planning a blood drive on a certain day at the county courthouse. Notifying the citizens in county D, E and F would be pointless because they live too far away from the site of the blood drive. And you want to reach adults, not little children or frail senior citizens. Plus you need healthy people, not those with communicable diseases or, for instance, drug abuse problems.

Now you've defined your potential blood donors (the people you want to take action so you can achieve your goal of increasing the blood supply). This is your AUDIENCE, and you have used criteria based on DEMOGRAPHICS.

Demographics is a way of dividing people into groups based on such factors as place of residence, age, socioeconomic level, marital status, gender, profession, race, educational level, etc. It's not always necessary to use all the variables; but the more you use, the more precisely you can isolate those people who have the potential to act in the manner you desire, and the better chance you have of isolating the most appropriate medium.

In our example, the demographics indicate we want to reach healthy adults who live in county A. That is our audience.

Case Study (continued)

We needed to reach everyone who might be considering a class at Glendale College. Many of those people would be graduating from high school in June. Others, in their 20s and 30s, would be "out there" somewhere. Still more would be working in the greater Glendale area, and, finally there were the retirees.

How to get the message to all those people? The mediums were diverse. For the teenagers, there were communiques to the counselors and PTA, and stories and ads in their high school newspapers and yearbooks as well as on local cable MTV and ESPN. For generation X, we relied on MTV, ESPN and CNN. We caught the business community with stories and ads in the newspapers, the Chamber of Commerce newsletters, and CNN. We tried some radio PSAs and also sent information to retirement homes. And we sent out postcards to all the area households.

It would have been nice to announce the message on our web site, but this situation arose before we had an exit on the information superhighway.

(Continued at the end of the next chapter....)

Related Web Sites

www.missouri.edu/internet-advertising-guide.html
www.nmresearch.com/index.htm
www.vidalsassoon.com

Medium/Channel

KABC radio engineer Brian Rumbaugh does some last-minute adjusting on the sound board for "The Dennis Prager Show."
Photo by Bill Lennert

The next step is to determine the best way to communicate with the audience. Not the message itself, but the channel or medium to be used. And the medium is determined by the demographics of the audience. Where are they? What do they watch, read, listen to on a daily basis?

If you wanted to reach county C blue collar males aged 18 to 25 with no college education, for example, you'd probably try to get your message on cable MTV and ESPN, into bars and pool halls, and maybe on a country music radio station. It would be a waste of time, money and effort to attempt to communicate with them through a university newspaper, wouldn't it? Or in a women's magazine? Chances are they'd never be exposed to your message.

To continue with our Red Cross example, what are the best mediums through which you can contact your audience—healthy adults who live in county A? Would a flyer at a convalescent hospital be appropriate? Or at a liquor store? An ad during a Saturday morning cartoon show? *Time* magazine?

Instead, how about local radio and TV public service announcements? The YMCA and YWCA? Church bulletins? Local newspapers? Libraries? The high school and community college? Local internet bulletin boards?

Common sense will take you a long way toward success. Use your head.

But before you begin to work out the plan's details, there's one more factor to consider: what's the budget? Keep reading.

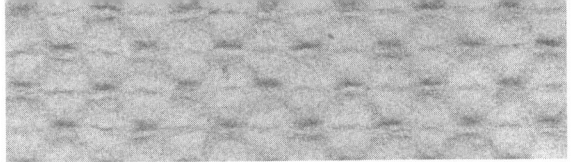

chapter twenty-two

EXERCISES

Name_____ **Date**_____

1. Continue with the imaginary organization you created for the Chapter 21 exercise. The goal has been set. Now it's time for demographics: define your audience and the appropriate mediums to reach it.

2. Do the same for the retail company.

3. Politician or rock star.

Chapter 23

The Campaign: Consider the Budget

Money. Money. Money. The design of your public relations campaign will be shaped by your budget, and there are many factors to take into consideration.

For instance, do you have an annual budget to which you must adhere? Is someone else going to tell you how much you can spend on the campaign, or do you have unlimited funds? Will it be your responsibility to decide what's cost-effective? How important is the success of the campaign: if it fails, will you be out of a job?

Once you've answered those questions, you should have a fairly clear idea of the dollar amount to be allotted to the campaign. The next step is to determine HOW to spend those monies.

Options and Costs

Advertising

A PR campaign may or may not include advertising. If print, broadcast or outdoor ads are necessary, complete details are available in Chapter 15. Direct mail is covered in Chapter 14. But for now, let's review and add some information.

If you represent a national company or client with broad-based recognition, you'll have to go country-wide with your campaign. And it's going to cost you. Big time. You'll have to purchase network TV air time, so count on spending millions of dollars there. You might want region-specific radio, major newspaper, region-specific billboard and general-interest magazine ads, too, so chalk up hundreds of thousands more. Yes, a national PR campaign can get very expensive.

Of course, if you have a nifty web site, that's an excellent and relatively inexpensive way to reach a worldwide audience. You also can mention your web address in advertising to lure people there.

But, if your interests are regional or local, you won't have to reach as many people and your costs could go down accordingly. We say COULD because you might elect to throw megabucks at the campaign anyway by blanketing the area with your message(s). TV, radio, newspaper, magazine and billboard ads will cost less simply because there will be fewer of them than you would need for a national effort. A local direct mail PR campaign also might be effective, with the cost varying substantially with the mailer's graphic quality.

TV news organizations tape satellite feeds for later broadcasting. This is KTLA's tape playback room.
Photo courtesy of the Daily News of Los Angeles

A regional campaign also allows you to be more specific when targeting your audience, which can pare down the numbers considerably. Put your ads on radio stations that attract the demographic audience you seek. Or your billboards in only one part of town. Or send your mailers just to specific zip codes. Or use ads only on local cable TV. In fact, you may be able to eliminate ads in several media if you're wise about the habits of your target audience.

Public Service Announcements

We discussed PSAs in depth in Chapter 13. If your budget does not allow for extensive media ads, PSAs might be the perfect solution. They cost nothing except time and effort. Be aware, however, that it's difficult to conduct a national campaign using PSAs. Radio isn't national, so you'd have to contact every station across the country. And TV networks seldom run PSAs—at least not at an hour when most people are awake. So, PSAs are more of a tool for regional efforts.

Measuring

One of the hidden costs of a PR campaign is the budget for measuring results. If your effort requires a public opinion survey to determine the effectiveness of the plan, and if you don't have an in-house department to handle the poll, then you'll have to hire someone to do it. The fee will depend on the scope of the survey. It should be noted that a web site can automatically register every "hit," but it doesn't tell you how well the page was received.

Product/Client Visibility

Another part (or all) of your PR campaign might include getting your client published or on talk shows, or your brand name visible in the latest movie, or a positive mention of your company on a TV sitcom.

This might or might not cost money, depending on the circumstances. You might have to wine and dine some people. You might have to give gifts (including your product). You might have to pay a promotional fee to get your client, product or organization shown or mentioned in the electronic media or in films. Print journalists generally eschew direct gifts or entertainment, but in the movie industry that comes with the territory.

Free, Free, Free

Of course, the ideal way to conduct a PR campaign is to get lots of positive media coverage. If the message is interesting enough, and you're persuasive enough, this is the most cost-effective (free) method.

Bringing it All Together

A PR campaign usually consists of a combination of advertising, direct mail, client visibility, web site, PSAs and media coverage—in decreasing order of cost.

You will have to decide how much (if anything) you want to spend, based on the importance of the message, the scope of the campaign and how narrowly the target audience can be identified.

Case Study (continued)

The budget is always a factor in our campaigns, and this case was no exception—especially since we had to use a variety of media outlets to reach everyone.

By cost, the least expensive (free) items were the messages to the counselors, PTA and retirement homes, the newspaper articles (local, high school and Chambers of Commerce) and the PSAs.

Next came the ads in the high school newspapers and yearbooks. These always are cost-effective. Sometimes a whole page is only $200.

Then there were the ads on cable MTV, ESPN and CNN. As we mentioned in the advertising chapter, these 30-second spots are $15 to $30. In this case we ran them several weeks at a time, so the overall price was close to $3,000.

We ran some local newspaper ads, and a quarter-page display averaged about $700. That's not particularly cost-effective, but community leaders (frequently opinion leaders) read the local papers.

And, finally, we sent out postcards to area households. Chapter 14 details those costs.

The campaign price was close to $10,000. But it should be remembered that California community colleges, at least at that time, received funding based on enrollment. I believe the figure was close to $3,000 per full-time student. So, if the message got us just three students, the campaign had almost paid for itself.

(Continued at the end of the next chapter. . . .)

Related Web Sites →

www.www.wellsfargo.com
www.mci.com
www.gm.com

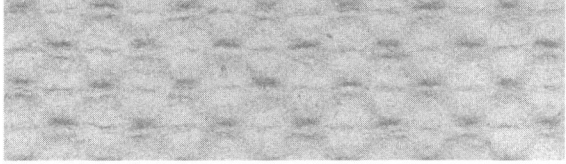

chapter twenty-three

EXERCISES

Name_____ **Date**_____

1. OK, you've got your imaginary organization; you've chosen a goal; you've defined your audience. Now, determine approximately how much you want to spend, based on the importance of the goal, the scope of the campaign and how narrowly you've identified your target audience. If appropriate, don't forget to factor in the cost of a public opinion poll. What mediums will you use? Are they expensive, moderately priced or free?

2. Same for the retail company.

3. Ditto for politician or rock star.

Chapter 24

The Campaign: Develop a Plan

Now that you have set realistic goals, defined the audience and determined the budget, you are ready to develop the plan.

It's sort of like fitting together the pieces of a jigsaw puzzle or working out the solution to a mathematical equation. All the variables ultimately must form a cohesive plan.

The Variables

You have a specific measurable goal, a target audience defined as narrowly as possible and X number of dollars to carry out your PR campaign.

What now?

The first step is to determine which media reach your target audience, and the next step is to see if you have enough money to use those media. If you don't have a sufficient budget, you'll need to be creative and find alternate routes for circulating your message.

Using the correct mediums (channels) is crucial to the success of your campaign. Placing an ad in the *L.A. Times* is not an effective way to reach New Yorkers, right? That may be obvious, but there are subtler variables to consider. For instance, would you have better luck getting to teens through a story in the town daily, with ads on local cable MTV, or using a PSA on a Top 40 radio station? Which channel would be the most effective and the least expensive?

Out of this process should come a list of the mediums you plan to use. If the campaign is complex, perhaps you'll have several target audiences and different mediums for each audience. For the average PR practitioner, however, there's just one message per campaign.

Matching Medium and Message

You've matched the mediums to the audience, and now you must match the mediums to the message.

What does this mean? It means different mediums require different packaging. For example, a TV commercial composed totally of printed words scrolling across the screen, with no audio, probably wouldn't be effective. If the people watching their sets wanted to read, they'd be reading instead of sitting in front of the TV. And what about those who have gone to the kitchen for a snack? They'll miss your message altogether.

Ergo, you have to package your message appropriately for each medium . . . and your audience.

Suppose your target audience is senior citizens, you want to tell them about free counseling for mortuary services, and you want to put an ad on local cable CNN. A rock video approach would not be appropriate for the audience or for the seriousness of the message. Actually, the scrolling words idea wouldn't be appropriate either, because that requires a visual capacity some elderly people might not have. Interference, remember?

When considering the web site medium, remember the demographics when creating the pages. Who has the necessary computer setup?

Bottom line: you must take into consideration all the intangibles that are not immediately obvious. Each message and its packaging should be designed specifically to match the medium and the audience.

The Message

Once you know which mediums you're going to use to reach the audience, and a preliminary concept of packaging that's appropriate for each medium, it's time to develop the actual message.

Usually this activity requires some sort of creativity on your part. What words and/or visuals will capture the audience members' attention? Try to put yourself in their shoes and think about their probable attitudes, which you can deduce in a general way from their demographics.

For example, if you wanted Generation X (people in their 20s and early 30s) to come to a particular clinic for free HIV screening, you probably should take a direct, no-nonsense approach because that seems to fit Gen X's overall attitude.

"How Safe Are You?" might be a good opening line, perhaps accompanied by a visual of one or two Gen Xers upside down or whirling out of control. "Your Life Depends on Knowing the Answer" could be an effective second line. Then, emphasizing FREE and SAFE, go on to give details about test dates and the clinic's hours, location and phone number. You might encourage them to "bring along your significant other."

Since you're dealing with one clinic, this would be a local campaign and a good prospect for ads on area cable MTV and ESPN. Use an alternative music score and MTV-like visual effects.

Flyers and posters placed in local Gen X hangouts also would be effective: nightclubs, fast-food franchises, the neighborhood gym, college campuses, record stores, the pool hall, etc. Be sure to use bright colors and interest-grabbing designs to attract attention. And allow time for convincing the proprietors of the above-mentioned locations to put up your posters and flyers. The subject matter and free services should help your cause.

This message would work on the radio, too, provided you utilize stations catering to the Gen X crowd. If it's an actual radio ad or a pre-recorded PSA, perhaps you could use the sound of ambulance sirens softly in the background. If station announcers will read the PSA, the message is almost as effective just on the verbal level. Don't forget, broadcasting mediums require repetition of specifics such as phone numbers.

The Plan

All the major components of your plan are now in place. You've identified the audience that, if convinced by your message, will alter its attitude or behavior so your goal will be achieved. You've chosen carefully the appropriate mediums to reach the target audience and you've designed and packaged what you hope is an effective message—all within your budget.

Measuring

There's just one other matter to take care of before you begin your campaign. How will you measure its effectiveness? An evaluation device or process must be built into the plan. Otherwise you might be doomed to repeat your mistakes.

It's easier to measure the effectiveness of a message encouraging your audience to take action. Did more people come to the clinic? Did more people sign up for classes? Did more people buy your product? Of course, you'll need "before" figures to compare with "after" figures, and arrangements need to be made to collect those statistics.

Another thing to consider—and this is where it can get complicated—is whether there were additional factors influencing your audience's behavior. For instance, did more people enroll in your firearms safety class because there had been a rash of burglaries in town? Or perhaps sales increased on your soft drink because the only competitor stopped manufacturing for a few weeks. Be alert to these possibilities when evaluating the plan.

Attitudinal changes are much more difficult to measure. Almost always this requires an opinion poll or a survey of some sort, and care must be taken to insure accuracy.

It's been said you can make a poll come out any way you want, and that's true. Some clients are not interested in an accurate indication of opinions. They will want you to phrase survey questions in a manner that almost predetermines the answers, and then they'll publicize those nefarious results for their own benefit. Eventually this policy will backfire, and you should encourage these clients to change their ways.

Others will be concerned about getting real information, and of course you'd rather be working for those folks. Nevertheless, if you're going to create a survey in-house rather than hire an outside consultant, you'll need to be very careful if you want accurate results. The slightest word or phrase can be misleading or have a subconscious effect on the person answering the questions. So can the order in which the questions are asked. So can the conditions under which the survey is conducted. So can a zillion other factors.

Social scientists believe random sampling of a portion of an audience's opinions can produce results that represent the entire audience's attitudes. There usually is a plus or minus error percentage, based on the size of the sample. Others disagree about the accuracy of surveys, and the issue is complicated by the fact that publicizing the results of a poll tends to make it a self-fulfilling prophesy. In addition, a number of people will answer questions the way they think they SHOULD answer rather than telling the truth about their attitudes.

When you design your survey, first you must decide if you're going to poll everyone or just a portion of the audience. If your audience is small, surveying all of them is a sure way to improve the odds of getting accurate information. But if it's a national audience, interviewing everyone is impossible, so you'll have to do a random sample. There are computer programs that can help you randomly choose participants.

Polls can be done by phone, by mail or in person, and each method has its drawbacks.

A phone survey will be affected by the time of day audience members are called. If no one's home, no one can answer questions; or perhaps someone answers but doesn't want to participate for whatever reason. If you place all your calls in the evening, for instance, your respondents probably will not include blue collar employees who work at night or Gen X members who might be out partying. Thus, the results of your poll will be skewed unless you phone during a variety of hours.

A survey by mail also is risky because the only respondents probably will be people who normally respond to questionnaires. That will skew your results.

Polling people in person has its drawbacks, too. Will some of them alter the truth by saying what they think you want them to say or what they think makes them sound

Case Study (continued)

The components of the plan were in place, so then it was time to actually create the ads, news releases, PSAs, post cards, and communiques.

Our message was simple: it was an early start alert. The language and visuals we employed depended on the demographics of the target audience. We also used the opportunity to tell everyone what Glendale College offers. I guess that was a secondary, but certainly not contradictory, goal.

Even though the TV campaign was aimed at teenagers, Gen Xers and the general public, we used the same commercial on all three cable stations. We created a generic ad we hoped would catch the attention of everyone. The PSAs and postcards also were of the generic persuasion.

Only the high school newspaper ads were really different because they were the key to such a tight target audience. I came up with a "Dear Dudes and Dudettes" approach, which was sort of cool at the time.

Messages going to the Chambers of Commerce, counselors and PTAs catered to those specific audiences and contained information each of them needed. High school counselors, for instance, would need to know the new, earlier registration dates.

We were ready to proceed.

(Continued at the end of the next chapter...)

Related Web Sites →
www.planetreebok.com
www.xerox.com
www.leejeans.com
www.sandiegozoo.org

good? Will you be stationed in a public place or will you go to people's homes? If you're in a public place, many will view you as a nuisance and refuse to participate, which, of course, skews the results. If you're going door-to-door, some people won't be home and others will refuse to respond.

As you can see, survey methods are just as important as the way you phrase your questions, and nothing is 100 percent foolproof or accurate.

Be sure to use the same survey, method and audience for your before-and-after polls to guarantee at least a relatively accurate comparison.

One final note on measuring: as we mentioned before, the web site automatically tallies the number of "hits" but does not reveal the audience's reaction to the site. However, if you advertise your web address in the media, the number of site hits will tell you how many people saw the original ad. And if you have an interactive page, you can ask for feedback.

Implementation

Now you're ready to implement the campaign. It's time to stop conjecturing and go to work. Of course, you might have to get the OK from your client or company executives before you proceed. But if you've planned carefully for all contingencies, and perhaps consulted with the boss along the way, you shouldn't have too much trouble convincing them.

chapter twenty-four

Name_____ **Date**_____

1. Continuing with this ever-expanding exercise, use the topics in this chapter as a basis for completing the PR plan for your organization.

2. For your retail company.

3. And for your politician or rock star.

Chapter 25

The Campaign: Implement Plan, Evaluate Effectiveness

OK, you're ready to implement the plan according to the timeline you've established. A timeline, by the way, should be an integral part of the presentation to your client and must include both your deadlines and the dates your creations will be received by the audience.

Here's an example:

Fundraiser Campaign Timeline
(Goal: increase ticket sales 25 percent for Benefit Ball)

July	1 -	Determine 25% increase from last year's numbers. Take publicity photos.
July	2 -	Buy time on local cable TV: CNN, USA, Discovery.
July	3 -	Write & send press release to Prescott Daily, Dakota Weekly, Chamber of Commerce Monthly. Include photos from last year's event, creative pictures of this year's chairpersons.
July	6 -	Story appears in Prescott Daily.
July	7 -	Story appears in Dakota Weekly.
July	15 -	Finish & send pre-recorded & hard copy PSAs to radio WWKK, WKKW, KWWW, KKWW, WWWW, KWWK.
July	20 -	Finish 30-second cable TV spot, deliver to cable operator.
Aug.	1 -	Buy ad space in Prescott Daily, Dakota Weekly. Story appears in Chamber Monthly.
Aug	2 -	Write & send press release with different emphasis, and calendar item, to Prescott Daily, Dakota Weekly, Chamber Monthly. Different photos.
Aug.	5 -	Calendar, second story appear in Prescott Daily.
Aug.	7 -	Calendar, second story appear in Dakota Weekly.
Aug.	8 -	Radio PSAs begin airing; 4 weeks
Aug.	9 -	Complete posters, flyers.
Aug.	10 -	Put up posters, flyers at beauty parlors, nail salons, gift shops, boutiques, selected stores.

> ### *Fundraiser Campaign Timeline (continued)*
> Aug. 12 -   TV spot starts airing; 3 weeks.
> Aug. 15 -   Send calendar item to radio stations.
> Aug. 25 -   Ad in Prescott Daily.
> Aug. 26 -   Ad in Dakota Weekly.
> Aug. 27 -   Ad in Prescott Daily.
> Aug. 29 -   Ad in Prescott Daily.
> Aug. 31 -   Ad in Prescott Daily.
> Sept. 1 -   Send creative photos & detailed cutlines to Prescott Daily, Dakota Weekly.
>   Calendar, second story appear in Chamber Monthly.
> Sept. 2 -   Ad in Dakota Weekly, Prescott Daily.
> Sept. 3 -   Photo spread appears in Prescott Daily.
> Sept. 4 -   Photo spread appears in Dakota Weekly, ad in Prescott Daily.
> Sept. 5 -   Prepare survey for Benefit Ball attendees.
> Sept. 10 -   Benefit Ball.
> Sept. 12 -   Compare attendance with last year, evaluate surveys.

Effectiveness

Did it work? In order to avoid repeating errors, and to help you design an even better plan next time, it is necessary to evaluate the effectiveness of the campaign.

In the example cited above, it would be easy to simply compare ticket sales. That would tell you if your plan was successful, but it wouldn't reveal HOW it worked. And that's why you need a carefully-crafted, simple survey to be filled out by everyone attending the charity event. The questionnaire would ask how the participant found out about the ball and would list all the alternatives—including word of mouth. Respondents could check off every applicable category, and then you'd know which mediums were the most successful in reaching your target audience.

The next step would be to compare the cost of each medium with its success rate. For instance, if only a small percentage checked off newspaper ads (expensive), you'd know that wasn't a cost-effective medium for increasing the event's ticket sales. And if lots of people heard the radio PSAs (free), you'd know that was a very cost-effective medium. Next year: Fewer newspaper ads (completely discontinuing them might result in fewer STORIES, which attract more attention than ads) and more emphasis on radio PSAs.

Many public relations campaigns are far more complex and require a great deal of evaluation and computation to determine a plan's effectiveness. Fortunately, complicated campaigns usually are carried out by the larger firms or by a big department within a company—which means there are sufficient numbers of employees to implement the plan.

Case Study (continued)

Our timeline strategy was simple: hit 'em early and then hit 'em again.

High school newspaper articles and ads, obviously, had to be placed in the spring. Almost everything else was done in May and then again in early July. The only thing we didn't repeat was the postcards.

Did it work? Yes.

We had no special measuring device in place except for the obvious one: students applied and registered a month earlier than usual. Was there a drop in enrollment because people didn't know we were starting early? No.

Was the campaign worth the effort and money? Definitely.

Related Web Sites

⟶

www.bud.com
www.budweiser.com
www.saturncars.com
www.pacbell.com

chapter twenty-five

EXERCISES

Name_____ **Date**_____

1. Devise a timeline for your organization's PR plan.

2. Do the same for your retail company.

3. And your politician or rock star.

Section Four

Crisis Management

Crisis Management: How to Prepare

As your institution's public relations expert, how do you prepare for a disaster that could strike at any moment? The most important thing to remember is you cannot prepare alone. Your company or organization should be encouraged to develop two types of crisis management plans—one for a natural disaster and one for the image-damaging disaster—and all personnel should know their roles.

Preparing in General

We noted in Section I the importance of cultivating professional relationships with reporters and encouraging an understanding of the media among your institution's co-workers. If you have met these goals with any degree of success, your job during a disaster will be much easier.

The first step in preparing for disasters in general is to make sure your company or organization has viable plans in place and everyone knows what to do. In a natural disaster, your role is only part of the program; but in an image-damaging disaster, your role is key.

The List

In either case, priority one for you is THE LIST. Make sure you continuously update your list of media phone and fax numbers and e-mail addresses, with contact names wherever possible, and keep a copy with you at ALL times. Include the PIOs for local police and fire.

You also should have home phone numbers for your institution's major officials. In addition, reporters, city desks, assignment editors and wire services should know your name and home phone number. And, finally, all employees should be informed that you need to be notified immediately when an emergency of any kind occurs —be it physical or potentially image-damaging.

The Natural/Physical Disaster

Disaster-preparedness is a topic of great seriousness for most companies, and you need to make sure your organization's contingency plan for a natural disaster properly includes your duties.

The purposes of having an official spokesperson are twofold: to give the media a reliable, agreeable contact to coordinate and issue accurate information, and to keep the press satisfied and out of the way of working police and fire personnel. If you do your job well, your efforts will be much appreciated by everyone.

The Team

Typically, disaster plans for the workplace follow certain guidelines. Key personnel have specific responsibilities, such as communicating instructions to employees, first aid, assessing structural damage, communication with police and fire officials, overseeing evacuation, making decisions, and media relations. Usually a small "disaster team" is predesignated to meet in the command center, which will be the hub for all communications. Each member of the team should have a back-up designee; and several locations should be predetermined for command centers, based on different contingencies.

The institution's official spokesperson—that's you—MUST be an integral part of the disaster team. Information must start flowing to you as soon as an emergency occurs, and you'll need to consult frequently with other members of the team. Everyone should understand media relations are your responsibility and it is your task to deliver OFFICIAL statements to the press. Of course, any employee is free to speak to reporters about personal (unofficial) observations and opinions.

It should be emphasized that during an emergency everyone is under stress—including reporters. Your job is to assist the media so members of the press can deal with just one official spokesperson. That means you must be accessible, cooperative, truthful, speedy, articulate and knowledgeable. Being physically and mentally prepared will help you perform under pressure, too.

Police/Fire Officials

It also is the spokesperson's duty to pre-establish communication links with police and fire department Public Information Officers (PIO), sometimes called Community Information Officers (CIO). Know who to contact and how to do it in the most expedient manner. During a disaster, you will need to establish ground rules for media access to the site, and you will need to be updated on injuries, structural damage, progress in bringing the emergency under control, etc.

In addition, you (and your designee or assistant) must have an official pass that will get you through police and fire lines in case an event happens while you are away from the office. The pass should be issued by the police, should carry your photo, and should be site-specific.

The Kit

If THE LIST is crucial for disaster-preparedness of both kinds, THE KIT is especially important for physical or natural emergencies. Your disaster kit should be kept in a safe place in your office. If funds allow, duplicate kits should be placed at the predetermined possible command centers, another kept in your car, and still another in the car of your assistant/designee.

The disaster kit, housed in an easily-transported cloth bag with straps or plastic box with handles, should contain the following:

The Kit

1. Instructions: a How-to Guide on dealing with the media during a disaster - for your assistant or designee.

2. The List (updated!).

3. Several notebooks of various sizes: You will need small pads for taking notes and larger ones for composing quick statements.

4. Pens, pencils, and a small pencil sharpener.

5. Cell phone. Or roll of dimes: You may need to use a pay phone.

6. Ten copies of fact sheets with pertinent information about your company or organization: To hand out to reporters on request.

7. Flashlight: Handy in many situations.

8. Masking Tape: To mark camera areas, or put up signs, etc.

9. Lighter, Swiss Army knife and small first aid kit: Standard survival items.

10. Quart of bottled water: For your needs. You might want to include a small amount of non-perishable, easily opened food.

11. Tennis shoes: Good shoes or high heels are a hindrance during a physical disaster. What if you have to walk on broken glass or climb over something?

12. Sweater, jacket or light blanket: In case it gets cold.

13. A beeper.

14. Something easily-seen that identifies you as the PIO/official spokesperson. Fire department PIOs frequently wear a hard hat with large PIO letters on it, and you could do the same. Other options are a large, colorful arm band with PIO on it, or a larger-than-usual and colorful badge/name tag with "PIO."

Other Preparations

In addition to the above, and if it's feasible, try to have the designated command centers equipped with phones, fax, computer with printer, small copier, water, first aid kit, and perhaps even a small microwave oven. Also, if funding is available, a fax or computer with fax-modem in your home and a phone in your car would be most helpful.

And, in case a disaster occurs on a weekend or at night, be sure to keep The List with you at all times. In addition, your assistant or designee should be trained or at least familiarized with proper procedures for dealing with the media in an emergency situation.

You can prepare a disaster plan, but you can't plan when it's going to happen.

Image-Damaging Disaster

In some ways, an incident or situation with the potential to damage your company's image can be worse for your organization than a natural disaster. The public will sympathize or at least be neutral if, for instance, part of your office complex is destroyed in a fire. But if your institution is a large medical center, for example, and it is discovered your noted pediatrician is molesting his patients, then you have BIG trouble.

To prepare for the image-damaging disaster, cultivating professional, trusting relationships with reporters is of prime importance. If the media see you and your organization as being open and truthful, with nothing to hide, chances are the press will tend to give you the benefit of the doubt when something AWFUL happens. If journalists already know you have integrity, they will be less suspicious and more inclined to accept your word. You can offer background or off the record information to help them understand. Of course, the story will be printed and aired, but the media will be less inclined to drag your company through the mud . . . and in the long run that means less dirt on your institution's face.

Another important factor in preparing for this type of disaster is:

Communication within your organization.

All employees should know that at the first hint of anything amiss, your office must be notified and given full details. If you are out of the office, efforts must be made to reach you or your assistant or designee.

If you have prepared well, reporters will contact you when something like this happens. But occasionally the press will go to other sources within your company. To prepare for this possibility, a short list—with you at the top—of company officials should be prepared in advance and circulated to all departments with instructions to refer media inquiries to those designated experts. Of course, any employee is free to talk to the press, but not as an official spokesperson.

You must be familiar with current federal and state laws regulating the release of information about personnel or clients. Many times the image-busting crisis is based on the activities of employees, and you need to know where to draw the line legally. While you're cultivating professional relationships with the media, make sure reporters also are familiar with the laws.

Of course The List will be necessary to contact the media once something of this nature takes place. If your institution's officials have not kept you up to date, you might find out about a situation FROM the media when they call to inquire about it. This can be embarrassing, but you'll just have to be honest. Tell reporters you'll get right back to them, and then start scrambling for the information they need.

The best policy for dealing with the media under any circumstance is honesty. And this situation is no exception. Tell the truth and don't try to hide anything. Remember the Tylenol pills laced with cyanide? The company came forward immediately, warned the public and asked for all pills to be returned. Today the company is still in business and doing extremely well. That PR exec made the right call.

You should know your local press well enough to recognize who is competing against whom. If only one journalist contacts you, act accordingly and notify the competition. Keep all the reporters up to date on the latest developments and don't play favorites. The only exception would be if a reporter has a true exclusive in the making, and in that case you'd have to use your best judgment.

Again, be sure you don't release information illegally. For instance, if the company suspects an employee is embezzling and the press gets wind of it, then you can say the company is investigating the possibility of embezzlement. But you can NOT release the name or position of the suspect. Conversely, if an employee has been ARRESTED and charged with embezzlement, that is a matter of public record and it can be released. However, you cannot discuss the details of the case until it is settled.

Both at Once

Sometimes there are crises that contain elements of both the natural disaster and the image-damaging disaster. Two examples come to mind:

The bomb in Centennial Park during the 1996 Atlanta Olympics, and, just a few days earlier, TWA's flight 800 that exploded off Long Island.

Talk about consecutive PR nightmares.

The TWA explosion had the potential to damage the airline's reputation. But two things its PR experts did get through to the public: the fact that TWA had an excellent record, and the fact that TWA held memorial services in several cities for the victims' families and friends.

As for the Atlanta Olympics, the event was a PR fiasco in many ways. If public relations people were on the job, there was little evidence of it. It appeared there was no PR component in the crisis management plan. No person wearing a PIO helmet ventured into the camera's glare.

The bomb was not the only problem in Atlanta. Nothing makes reporters unhappier than constantly being inconvenienced. And disgruntled journalists eventually report those problems to their audience. Although NBC, perhaps fearing a drop in the ratings, did not say much about the following snafus, the print media certainly did, and so did other networks.

For example, several international broadcast consortiums allegedly demanded their money back from the organizing committee because of malfunctioning computer equipment. According to print journalists covering the Games, reporters were subjected to almost constant disrespect and disorganization. There were widespread reports of horrendous transportation problems and oppressive heat. And one newspaper columnist wrote about his typical morning routine: brush teeth, drink coffee, evacuate building due to bomb threat.

It was a classic case of PR ignorance: underestimating the importance of media relations.

Compare the Atlanta event to the 1984 Olympics in Los Angeles. There, the PR/sports information people were experienced pros who knew how to keep reporters happy by facilitating what was needed, when it was needed. The end result was great PR for the city of Los Angeles. (To be fair, L.A. didn't have terrorists, transportation crises or weather problems; but the media relations effort truly was superior.)

A little common sense goes a long way.

Plan ahead.

Case Study

Glendale College does have a natural disaster plan, and there's a large PIO component.

(You'll recall the image-damaging crisis is covered in the Media Relations Guidelines.)

When the college organized its disaster-preparedness plan, many departments contributed ideas, and a task force honed it down to a workable format. There's a permanent phone tree (people designated to call other people) in place for any kind of emergency. Supplies are stored away. Emergency vehicles have been purchased. But are we ready?

A campus-wide drill to test the newly prepared disaster plan took place one afternoon near the end of the spring semester. The scenario was an explosion and toxic spill in the chemistry lab, with many injuries. Several buildings were evacuated. Five key people (including the PIO) had to go to the pre-determined command post, and certain health-care staff and team leaders had other assigned tasks. Theatre arts students played the injured victims.

At that time I happened to be teaching both print and broadcast journalism. For their final exam, I had all the students meet me in the journalism lab at a predetermined time—with camcorders, cameras and notepads ready. When the alarm sounded, I told them what was happening and then hurried to the command post. My students served as the media in the drill. Cool, no?

Anyway, some things went smoothly. For example, the media gave me no trouble at all! But other things did not go as well. We discovered we were missing many items, including enough functioning walkie-talkies, medical carts, blankets, etc. There were communication problems. The command post didn't know where the triage area was.

After all the excitement, the task force reconvened the following week to discuss what had happened and start making revisions to the plan.

Now we're better prepared (after all, that was the point of the drill), but we probably should practice some more. If the major earthquake predictions are correct, Glendale College could be standing on future beachfront property.

Related Web Sites

⟶

www.twa.com
www.olympic.org

chapter twenty-six
EXERCISES

Name_____ **Date** _____

1. You work for a large, well-known company that produces recyclable plastic. A by-product of the manufacturing process is a small amount of toxic waste, which is supposed to be discarded through contracts with disposal companies. An environmental group comes to the CEO with a disturbing story—evidence that your supervisor in charge of dealing with the disposal companies is pocketing the money designated for that purpose and dumping the toxic waste in a local river. Your CEO investigates immediately and discovers the story is true. As the company's public relations expert, what do you do? Write a short essay.

Name_____   **Date** _____

2. Two police officers from your city near the Mexican border chase a truckload of apparently illegal immigrants for several hours—at speeds up to 100 miles per hour—until the vehicle runs out of gas. By this time the chase has attracted the attention of newscopters, who hover overhead recording the conclusion of the activity. As the truck comes to a stop, the 20 people in it leap out and start running away. The two police officers grab two of the people, and when they fail to comply with English commands to lie down, hit them quite a few times with their batons. The newscopters are broadcasting live, and the complaints immediately start pouring in from various ethnic and civic organizations. As the city's public relations official, you have a nightmare on your hands. What should you have done to prepare for this contingency, and what do you do now? Short essay.

Name_____   **Date**_____

3. Your well-known movie star client has been arrested for possession of drugs and driving under the influence. The information goes on the police report, of course, and the media finds out and airs the information. Your client has had a clean record up to now and he is released the next morning. You advise him to seek drug counseling. Three days later he is discovered sleeping on the floor of a stranger's home, and he's arrested again. You bail him out and insist on drug rehab. He goes, but two days later he "escapes" and is once again arrested for drug possession and driving under the influence. This time he goes to jail, with no bail. It's the publicist's nightmare, because your client's behavior has gone beyond even Hollywood's tolerance. What should you have done, and what should you do now? Short essay.

Chapter 27

The PR Role in a Natural Disaster

Preparation

When a natural or physical disaster occurs at the workplace, certain procedures should be followed in dealing with the media. Whatever your title—be it Public Relations Director, Public Information Officer, Vice President of Marketing, or whatever—you should be prepared to assume the responsibilities of the official company or organization spokesperson.

As was noted in Chapter 26, the media need a single spokesperson from the disaster site who is accessible, truthful, articulate, knowledgeable, experienced, cooperative and can coordinate information from others and dispense it to the media.

In preparation for such an event, the designated spokesperson should know the quickest way to communicate with (1) local police and fire department PIOs to coordinate efforts and (2) designated on-site persons who will report damage, casualties, etc. to the spokesperson. In addition, the spokesperson should have an up-to-date list of phone and fax numbers for local Associated Press and regional metrowires, any area news wires, local newspaper city desks, and assignment desks at area TV stations and radio news stations.

What to Do

If there is time for just a few contacts, the wire services would take priority because all the media subscribe to at least one. The message sent should include information about media access to the site, the location of the command center, and the name of the spokesperson (who should be wearing something to designate him/her as the public information officer).

During a disaster, the media needs facts, opportunities for still photographs and opportunities for video. In addition, the spokesperson should facilitate safe media access to the site, designate reasonable camera angles and provide interviewees.

If these things are not provided, the media could feel thwarted and the situation could degenerate, probably resulting in the release of false and confusing reports to the public. As a local TV news person once said, "Rambo-esque reporting isn't necessary if information is made available in an organized manner."

Accordingly, by the time the media have reached the site, the spokesperson/PIO should be prepared with as much of the following information as possible:

INFORMATION TO GATHER

1. Physical damage to structures and financial losses.

2. Current status of the emergency (are there toxic fumes in the area, is the fire still out of control, has everyone been evacuated, are the hostages still inside the building, etc.)

3. Number of injuries.

4. Types of injuries.

5. Where casualties have been taken.

6. Number of dead.

7. Causes of death.

8. Probable causes of the disaster.

9. Where camera persons can stand.

10. Where reporters and camera crews can NOT go.

11. Names, proper spellings and titles of those in command at the site and those the media wish to interview.

12. Facts about your company or organization such as how many employees, what the company does, who the officers are, etc.

The PR person should remain at the command center and continue to synthesize and dispense information until the media's needs have been met. At all times, the PIO should be cooperative and helpful.

Other Kinds of Disasters

There may be occasions when the "disaster" really isn't a disaster but rather a situation where you need to get a message to the public in a hurry. For instance, suppose you work for Amtrak, and overnight a large mudslide has covered the tracks between two major cities. The trains won't be running until the tracks are cleared the next day, and you need to get the word out to commuters. What to do? THE LIST, of course. Phone or fax everyone so the information has a better chance of wide circulation.

There's also the possibility of a huge natural disaster—like an earthquake or hurricane—involving not just your organization but a wide area. In that case you'd be working with national as well as local media and coordinating your efforts with police and fire department PIOs and representatives from hospitals, the Red Cross, and maybe even the National Guard. Pre-established communication links are the key here, and a cellular phone would be worth pure gold.

KCAL technical director Rick Ricksen in the control room, where he'd be pushing buttons to air live
microwave feeds coming from the scene of a disaster.
Photo courtesy of the Daily News of Los Angeles

What to Do if You're Not There

Natural and physical disasters frequently happen at the most unexpected and
inconvenient times—on weekends, or in the middle of the night, or perhaps when
you're on vacation. Unless you're completely out of touch with your company or
organization (in which case your assistant or designee will step in and use the Disaster
Kit's How-to Guide for dealing with the media during an emergency), you are still the
official spokesperson and must act accordingly.

If your Disaster Plan is working, you will be contacted by whomever is responsible
for reaching you during an emergency. Barring that, you may be called by the media, or
you may hear about the disaster in some other way. In any case, you must act immediately.

First, establish contact with your company's command center, as well as police and
fire officials, and gather as much information as you can.

Second, contact the media and pass along the facts of the situation.

Then, if you are close enough in proximity, try to reach the site. You will have your
special police/fire credentials to get you through their lines, and you can proceed to the
command center.

If you are too far from the site to reach it in a timely manner, you will have to do
everything by phone or fax. This is much more difficult, but it can be done. Stay in
constant contact with whomever is designated by the police or fire captain at the site, or
with any company personnel on site, who can give you frequent updates. Then pass
along the information to the media. If the event is taking place in the middle of the
night, few reporters will be at the scene. In that case, your best bet would be the local
wire service.

The Drill

(Hypothetical Situation: During office hours, fire alarms begin to sound continuously in your company's 24-story building. Your PR office is on the second floor.)

1. Check your watch and write down the time. Call the office responsible for the building's maintenance and find out what is happening. (You are told there was a small explosion on the 19th floor and most of that floor is on fire. Some people are injured. All personnel in the building are being evacuated, and the fire department is on the way.) Write down the information and ask to be kept updated at the command center, which (it has been predetermined) will be the conference room on the ground floor as long as it is safe.

2. Call the fire department PIO and establish a communications link between the fire department and the conference room. Do the same with the police department PIO.

3. Speed is important! Gather your "Disaster Kit" (list of phone and fax numbers, several notebooks, pencils, pens, flashlight, bottled water, roll of dimes, fact sheets, masking tape, sweater or jacket, tennis shoes), put on your spokesperson badge, hat or armband, and take the stairs down to the command center in the conference room. The others in the predetermined Disaster Team also should be assembling there.

4. Take a notepad and pencil from the kit and go outside. Check in with the police or fire captain in charge and find out as much information as you can about structural damage, injuries, etc. Inform the captain the command center is in the conference room and establish a communication link. Consult about out-of-bounds areas for the media. Quickly take a look around for safe but reasonable camera angles and then return to the command center.

5. Contact the local wire service by phone, fax or e-mail. The message should be concise:

   "A fire caused by a small explosion of unknown origin has been burning since 2:15 p.m. on the 19th floor of the 24-story Acme Avis Co. at 2222 Main St. There are injuries, and employees are being evacuated. Police and fire officials are on the scene. The command center is the conference room on the ground floor, and media access is through the main lobby. The PIO on site is Kelly Smith and the phone number is 555-2222."

6. The media will have learned about the situation from the wire service or police and fire radios, and by now they'll be arriving outside. In fact, some reporters already may have found you in the command center. Go back outside and brief the media with all the information you have. Show camera crews the locations you have selected, and indicate the areas journalists may NOT go. Announce that you will continue coordinating and dispensing information from the command center, that you will do your best to answer all questions and provide requested data, and that you will arrange interviews with other company officials as needed.

7. Return to the command center and communicate with your sources in building maintenance, fire and police departments. Try to discover how many people have been injured and where they've been taken. What kinds of injuries—were they serious or not? What is the current status of the emergency? Is the fire being contained on the 19th floor, or is it spreading? Is anyone missing? How much structural damage has occurred? Is there a dollar estimate? Does anyone care to

Case Study

Since 1977, the closest Glendale Community College has come to a physical disaster was an accident that occurred off-campus. Here was the situation: I live 10 miles from campus and my office hours at that time began at 9 a.m. On a Tuesday morning at 8 a.m. I received a call at home from a local newspaper reporter who wanted to know if the college would be closed that day because of the overturned tanker truck and oil spill at a major intersection adjacent to the campus.

It was the first I'd heard of the incident and I promised to call the reporter back as soon as I got any information. I phoned the college, but the lines were all busy. I knew I had to find out if classes were cancelled for the day and immediately get that information to the broadcast media. We have 14,000 students and 1,000 faculty coming in from all over the Los Angeles area.

Eventually I got through to the campus police department, who informed me that city police and fire had blocked off the intersection and all streets for a mile in every direction. No cars would be allowed through (preventing access to the campus) until the oil spill had been eradicated. I called the college president and applied some pressure: a decision had to be made. I called the city fire PIO, but he wasn't sure how long the cleanup would take. Eventually the college administration made the decision to cancel classes, and I went to work on notifying the media.

This was before faxes, so I had to telephone everyone. I started with the wire services, then called the two all-news radio stations, then all the TV newsrooms. I did phone back the original newspaper reporter and continued to keep her apprised of the situation. I also called the other two papers that regularly cover the college.

Hopefully I helped a lot of students and faculty avoid a fruitless trip to an inaccessible campus. Of course, eventually I had to try to get to my office. I didn't have any kind of official police identification, so I had to do some fast talking and creative U-turns to get through police lines. Finally I was able to complete my task from the comfort of my own desk.

It's a good thing classes were cancelled, because the mess wasn't cleaned up until midnight.

Related Web Sites

www.redcross.org
www.fema.gov
www.naer.com

speculate on the cause of the explosion and fire? Update the press continuously, and provide information about the company as well.

8. From now on you must improvise. As long as you are prepared, you should be able to cope with any situation. Think about where the command center could be moved in case the location becomes unsafe. Stay in touch with your sources. Provide reporters access to the phones. If you notice any local media are missing, call or fax the information to them. If it looks like the situation could go on for awhile, you might think about ordering some food.

9. Try to keep your sense of humor.

10. If you discover your company is responsible for the explosion and fire—through negligence or whatever—do NOT withhold that information. The media will find out sooner or later; but if YOU disclose the information, chances are good there will be three desirable results:

A. The media will report facts rather than potentially more harmful hearsay and rumor.

B. Your company's public image will not be as tarnished because the organization will be perceived as open and honest rather than guilty of trying to cover up the incident.

C. When another image-damaging event occurs next month or next year, reporters probably will tend to give you and your company the benefit of the doubt because you have established your integrity and trustworthiness.

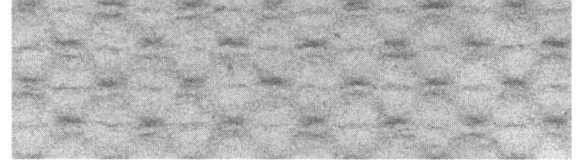

chapter twenty-seven
EXERCISES

Name _____ **Date** _____

1. You're the PR officer for a nuclear power plant. There's been a slight accident, and the staff is checking for radiation leaks. The accident itself is not yet under control, and it may be several hours before the event is contained. Write a short essay covering how you should handle the situation. Do you contact the media? When? What do you tell them?

2. As the vice president of public relations for a large chain of hotels, what should you do when a fire breaks out at the headquarters hotel, which is 45 stories high? Your office is on the first floor of that building, but the fire starts at 9 p.m. (in the middle of the building) and you're at home. Write a short essay.

Name_____ **Date** _____

3. The state of North Idaho has suffered a major earthquake, and your town—Elk's Foot—was the epicenter. Write an essay detailing what you should do, assuming you are the city's PR specialist.

Index

* An asterisk indicates that the subject is covered within chapter 18, which is on-line at http://www.coursewise.com/shelburne/